UNTETHERED

KATE ELIZEBETH NAGEL

Foreword by Lynn Schoener

BALBOA.
PRESS
A DIVISION OF HAY HOUSE

Balboa Press books may be ordered through booksellers or by contacting:

Balboa Press
A Division of Hay House
1663 Liberty Drive
Bloomington, IN 47403
www.balboapress.com
1 (877) 407-4847

Because of the dynamic nature of the Internet, any web addresses or links contained in this book may have changed since publication and may no longer be valid. The views expressed in this work are solely those of the author and do not necessarily reflect the views of the publisher, and the publisher hereby disclaims any responsibility for them.

The author of this book does not dispense medical advice or prescribe the use of any technique as a form of treatment for physical, emotional, or medical problems without the advice of a physician, either directly or indirectly. The intent of the author is only to offer information of a general nature to help you in your quest for emotional and spiritual well-being. In the event you use any of the information in this book for yourself, which is your constitutional right, the author and the publisher assume no responsibility for your actions.

Any people depicted in stock imagery provided by Thinkstock are models, and such images are being used for illustrative purposes only. Certain stock imagery © Thinkstock.

Printed in the United States of America.

ISBN: 978-1-5043-2734-3 (sc)
ISBN: 978-1-5043-2736-7 (hc)
ISBN: 978-1-5043-2735-0 (e)

Library of Congress Control Number: 2015901439

Balboa Press rev. date: 02/10/2015

CONTENTS

Part One
The House that Built Me

Part Two
The Fortress I Built

Part Three
Lowering a Drawbridge

Part Four
Untethered

To my dad,
David Carl Nagel

"This is love: to fly toward a secret sky, to cause a hundred veils to fall each moment. First, to let go of life. Finally, to take a step without feet." -- Rumi

FOREWORD

Most books within the how-to/self-help genre fall, for me, along a continuum. Anchored at one extreme are the experts, naturally gifted and inherently skilled, speaking solutions from a position of supremacy. The opposite point of this continuum is home base for the reformed, and they trust that the telling of their mighty struggle to mastery will serve as a mandate for their methodology. Whether a book promotes improvement by leading with head and strategic thinking, or by leaning on heart and personal story, every attempt to help and heal adds value. Rarely, however, does any book along this continuum tell the whole truth of transformation. You have in your hands one that does.

To create a work which resonates deeply enough with readers to evoke lasting change, an author has to jump this horizontal track of information and inspiration. To be sure, *Untethered* is a searing memoir of Kate Elizebeth Nagel's realization of the sinister roots of her addiction to work. It chronicles her courageous recovery from the legacy of sexual abuse and the subsequent suffocation of her spirit, by self and others. It is also a treasury of tactical guidance, not just for the workaholics among us but for anyone tethered inexplicably to a way of being that has ceased to serve them. The uncommon power of this book, however, is sourced from her intrepid travels along a vertical continuum. Her willingness to descend and rise, again and again, along this axis of shadow and light empowers us with a profound sense of how to orchestrate our own journeys, and find our way to our own liberating truths.

A core component of my executive coaching is devoted to clients in the shapeshifting terrain of transition, fine-tuning their inner GPS as they trek this "nowhere between two somewheres." Therefore, I rarely work with a person so clear at the outset about her purpose and process. Kate came to me in the final stages of crafting this book, and sought my support in staying on her ambitious schedule. We contracted around accountability, distraction management, and staying true to her still-emerging butterfly self. It was my assessment, and hers, that she was well on her way. We could not have predicted that our work together would call upon the degree of depth and creativity that it did.

More profound than any transition work I had undertaken with clients to date, Kate and I were called one blustery March day in 2014 to the task of transformation. With great care and collaboration, we said "yes." Something as yet invisible and inaudible wanted to be discovered, expressed, and integrated, and it had selected our container of coaching in which to reveal itself. Through the process of active imagination, she reoriented herself to an emerging aspect of her truth. It was unexpected, it was inconvenient given her goals, and it was a sacred experience for us both as we refocused our energies on this metamorphosis.

Speaking of metamorphosis–the "caterpillar to butterfly" transformation– pundits who point to the gossamer-winged wonder as a metaphor for change rarely describe in detail what happens in that cocoon. Within the silky and secure sanctum of the chrysalis, the caterpillar is sacrificing what it has been to enable what it will become, dissolving and digesting its own tissues. A glimpse inside wouldn't reveal a caterpillar sprouting wings, but instead, what appears to be an undifferentiated soup.

Highly organized groups of cells, however, known as imaginal discs, survive the digestive process. Back when that caterpillar was still developing inside its egg, it grew an imaginal disc for each of the adult body parts– eyes, wings, legs–that it would need as a mature butterfly. Although the caterpillar looks disintegrated, the imaginal discs remain. The discs use that protein-powered goo to fuel the rapid cell division required to form the fully-equipped and sublimely beautiful butterfly. In her surrender to a change process that wasn't finished with her, I witnessed Kate's imaginal discs at work. With resolve, integrity, and faith in her future emergence, she suspended the book project to dissolve into this new knowing, providing fuel for this iteration of her selving.

I believe that three communities in particular will benefit from the author's disciplined and repeated willingness to go into dimly seen spaces in her psyche, hold herself emotionally steady in the face of crippling fear, and bear the prolonged tension that deep change requires. I've studied and supported enough change to know that expanding self-awareness is the first step, but not the whole story. Kate has written *Untethered* for those of us in the helping professions, who want to learn more about the mystery of transformative change. She inspires us to sit with and grow the glimmer of awareness in those we serve, and provides guidance for leveraging that new knowing into different doing.

Twenty years of coaching in numerous corporate cultures has only reinforced my conviction that dysfunctional behavior is rarely about what it seems to be about on its face. We are seldom invited, however, on a guided tour of the hidden landscape of emotions, experiences, and assumptions that collude to influence a personality. Kate's generous transparency about her workaholism—the source and the symptoms—provides guidance for readers ready to examine their own voracious appetites for performing, approval, perfection, power, and/or control in their work roles and settings. Within the confines of a punishing schedule, largely self-inflicted and yet enforced by her clients and superiors, she committed her suffering self to the discipline of reflection. It saved her. Even if work is not your drug of choice, it is her intention that you'll be encouraged to explore the roots of whatever holds you back from happy.

Finally, Kate speaks to and for the survivors of sexual abuse, who are fully-functioning adults externally, but long to have a different internal experience of themselves. She offers not models or methodologies, but a deeply personal narrative detailed enough to provide the recognition, validation, and navigation so essential to healing, wholeness, and the reclamation of spirit. It is not meant to be a substitute for professional help, nor is it written for individuals currently being victimized. It is, however, a testimony to the richness and wonder that life can hold on the other side of this deep sadness.

In one of the more cryptic passages in the Gospel of Thomas, Jesus is reported to have said, "If you bring forth what is within you, what you bring forth will save you. If you do not bring forth what is within you, what you do not bring forth will destroy you." In *Untethered*, we have a vibrant endorsement of that enigmatic assertion. Kate did not deserve the losses, emotional betrayals, and violations to mind and body that she suffered, but they inhabited and held her spirit hostage for many years. She ultimately chose to "bring forth." As she did, her protracted adversity slowly revealed its powerful purpose. If you are in a season of "bringing forth," you could have no better companion.

If your impetus to read further is driven more by curiosity, or a desire for a riveting read, this book will intrigue and inspire. If inspiration prompts action, give in. We each have our own internal committees to tangle with, egoic dragons to slay on our way to a more open hearted, better understood, fully awake Self. A life with more light requires a courageous and compassionate examination of our shadows. May *Untethered* release in you an enthusiasm to embrace your work, for our world.

Lynn Schoener
Executive Coach
Cincinnati, Ohio

PREFACE

This is a story about letting go. I named the book Untethered because it's the one word that best describes what I did and how I now live. A tether is a restraint to hold something in place and limit its motion and movement. Although tethers can sometimes be used as safety measures, in all cases they are used to control or contain the limit of something.

I was tethered to an unknown force within me that was protecting me. In doing so, it was preventing me from having the life I wanted. This protective force was born of mechanisms and skills I had learned in order to survive a trauma-ridden childhood. I manifested those into destructive, addictive behaviors as an adult.

What was my addiction? Work. I used work as a barrier to protect myself from a life that I was simply too afraid to live. I found safety and fulfillment in work and became relentless in my pursuit of achievement and perfection. In relationships, I was guarded and afraid to trust. I used judgment and inflexibility to distance myself from the potential that someone or something could hurt me. I thought happiness was something I didn't deserve and was beyond my capacity.

In 2009, I made a deliberate choice to change the course of my life and find the root causes of those behaviors. I wanted to know exactly how I came to be who I was. I wondered if it was possible to redirect my insatiable, unhealthy appetite for work into a passionate, purpose-driven life based on my heart's ideals and intentions. The journey took me down many trails. There were moments when the terrain was slippery and treacherous, yet I continued my pursuit.

As I experienced this transformative process, I used writing as a medium to engage, explore, and heal. The first essence of this book started in 2010. The initial drafts appeared as pages of journals, notes, and readings. Four years later, on a cold winter Cleveland night as I evolved my writings into the first draft of this book, a quiet inner voice surfaced. The voice took the form of a child within me. She had a story to tell and she made an unexpected request of me. She asked me to let her tell it exactly as she wanted it told. I yielded. I allowed her to tell, and she led me down a dark and at times frightening path to the root of every protective barrier and mechanism that lived within me.

This is the story I had no idea was within me, and I had no idea I would tell; yet it is the one I was meant to tell. It is the story of how I let go, and emerged... untethered.

ACKNOWLEDGMENTS

"All you need is faith and trust... and a little pixie dust." -- Tinkerbell

I am adding one more thing to Tinkerbell's equation... the love, support and kindness from friends, family, and colleagues. There are many amazing people who helped me tell this story. My gratitude for you all is beyond measure.

To Lisa Willson, a sister, best friend, and gentle, loving ear and shoulder. I would not have survived this past year were it not for your unconditional kindness, unwavering support, and ongoing assurance that I could do this. Thank you for making me laugh on the days I didn't want to, helping me find and hear and see what I needed to on these pages, and reminding me that childhood friends are not only the best, they are priceless.

To Lynn Schoener, a guide, intuitive soul, friend, and fellow collector of hearts. Thank you for your many gifts. Active Imagination empowered me to conquer the final battles within me and interact safely with my greatest fears and unknowns. You created the space and allowed me to explore and embrace the peaceful power that emerges when mind, spirit, and heart converge for one common goal, love.

To Eileen Terry, more than a coach, a friend, and postulate of the spirit's limitless potential. Thank you for helping me reframe the absolute worst within me, and shift my perspective so that I may experience and embrace the brilliance of life through a lens of possibility.

To Christopher, my mirror, shadow, and muse. I became a better writer the night you told me you wouldn't read my book. I am not sure if you were an ending or beginning; but you touched my heart nonetheless, and your influence on me during this process was far greater than you may know. Thank you for reminding me encouragement and support comes in many forms, and sometimes when and where it's least expected.

To my anal-retentive, nitpicky editorial team, this story is richer because you all touched it with your hearts (and red pens). Leonie Elizabeth, thank you for helping me structure the story and smooth out the edges. I am honored to have shared your first steps as an editor with mine as an author. Susan Poole, I am grateful that life re-united our friendship at this moment, and we have the opportunity to know each other now, as we both journey into the world of writing. Lisa, Lynn, Eileen, and Susan, thank you for being thoughtful, honest, and constructive friends. You read all the rough stuff, asked me to dig deeper, and then believed in me that I could do it. Thank you Cindy Field Thatcher for combing these pages with a careful eye and loving heart. Last by no means least, Jen Smith. Thank you for taking the final steps with me as this manuscript became a book. Your thorough focus and gentle spirit brought a final, beautiful spark to this story.

To Scotty Jo, you are an amazing friend and guide. To Sean O'Reilly, thank you for being a supportive friend and helping me stay grounded as I reach for the stars. To Allison Bates for being a great listener and friend. To Bill Willson for sharing your photographic talents and capturing the essence of my story so beautifully. To Phaedra for encouraging my creative spirit and helping my heart find its way back to the playground. To Rita who joined Ellen, Faith, Sara, Lorne, Charles, Polly, and Kim on the beach, and showed me what unconditional trust feels like. To my fellow Falcons, the Fall 2013 CIT Class, Pam and Toni McLean, and everyone at the Hudson Institute. To my doctors and healers for saving my life, over and over again.

To a man in Chicago and one in Sedona who stepped out of the dark long enough to show me the light. To two men named John who were the first to hear my truth and set beautiful, caring examples. To my uncle, I miss you. To my grandpa for giving me the twinkle in my eye, the spark of my intuition, and the loving way honor to my great-grandmother, Elizebeth. To my dad, thank you for giving me my smile, kindness, and heart. I honor you with this story and am proud to be your daughter.

INTRODUCTION

I looked at them both and asked simply, "What do you want me to do here?" I had reached an impasse with my writing. Specifically, writing this book. I had imagined how it would go, and up to this point, it had played well. I was eager to see how it ended. At this moment, however, I was given pause. Somehow, something seemed different. I was different. Everything was different. I stared out over the red rocks of Sedona. I paused as my gaze rested upon Cathedral Rock. My mind briefly revisited the past five years, the many hikes up that rock, and all I accomplished within myself. I shifted back and looked at the two of them sitting there.

I sat there and watched them. Like two peas in a pod, yet they couldn't be more different. I met her first, the seven-year-old, my heart. She surfaced about five years ago during my first trip to Sedona. We had spent a good bit of time together. She has a spontaneity and zest for life. She is quite sensitive and can be timid and shy. She doesn't like to be the center of attention. She is happiest when she is playing and laughing. In this moment, she is animated, fidgety, and a bundle of silly energy, much like you would expect from a happy little girl on a warm summer day. The older one, the ten-year-old, we had just met. She was definitely more serious as you would expect the ego, the protector to-be. In that same moment, she seemed a bit distracted and yet quite focused at the same time. She was more contemplative and deliberate in her thoughts and quite cautious in her acts. She always had been. While there was a softening in her that I had just recently noticed, she stood firm in her conviction, believing in herself most of all.

She looked at her hands and considered. I could see her big blue eyes in deep, deep thought. When we first met, one of the things she revealed to me was that her hands had been tied her whole life. She was unable to move. She felt helpless, confused, afraid, and alone. She couldn't tell me which emotion she felt more than others. She felt them all the same, and to the greatest degree one could ever imagine.

She is quite bright. She can be a bit bossy. She looked up and said, "You have to tell the story the way I want you to. No matter how you think you wanted to tell it, now, you have to tell it this way. Now that you know what I know, you have to tell it." Her tone was confident, stoic, and adamant.

I glanced at the seven-year-old to hear what my heart had to say. She half-shrugged her shoulders and said, "Let her do it her way, you know it's what she wants. I'm okay with it too. Just tell it, please, so we can go play. And I get to pick the swing I want first today because she got to go first last time."

I smiled and considered what they said. My eyes went to the older one. I had only known her distinctly for about ten weeks, and yet she had always lived within me. She was the strength, courage, and fight that had carried me through my life. Together, we had sustained horrors beyond imagination. Yet, a choice was made that she would be the one to carry those memories in the deepest levels of my subconscious, the darkest corners of my soul. She took it upon herself to keep these memories blocked out and blacked out. She did this to protect me. She did this to protect the heart, the seven-year-old. In doing so, she had carried a burden within her far greater than any ten-year-old should ever have to bear. A burden far greater than any human being should ever have to experience. One night in late March 2014 she let go, and she let me remember. She unchained us from decades of confusion and darkness. She unhinged our memories in a way that almost instantly made our life make complete and total sense for the first time in nearly forty years. She set us free. Now, it's time for me to do the same for her.

I asked her if she was afraid and she said, "Yes, aren't you?" I nodded, *yes*. She stared at me intently and I could see the tears in her courageous, determined eyes.

I nodded and said, "Okay, we'll tell it your way." I glanced over at the younger one, growing impatient by the minute, and anxious to get things going. I asked the older one, "Should we let her go first?" She heaved a heavy sigh, and said, "Yes, she should go first, she was first." I considered them both. I watched the seven-year-old sit up in her chair as she prepared to share her story. The ten-year-old sat back with an ever-watchful eye over that sweet, tender heart. My heartbeat with the bubbly energetic magic of that seven-year-old and my ego held firmly in the grasp of that ten-year-old. And I carried both delicately and definitively as I sat in front of my laptop and continued writing our story.

PART ONE

The House that Built Me

From the seven-year-old, the heart:

My name is Kate, and I'm seven years old. I live in Ohio and I go to Westerly School. I'm in second grade and I'm old enough that I can walk to school all by myself, with my brother.

I like my school. It has a big playground in the back and one in the front, too. The one in the back has swings and I like to swing most of all. I can go very high, and I never get afraid. I always know how to stop and I like the times when I jump before the swing stops. I can jump far and it feels like I fly. Sometimes I fall, but mostly I fly. I can almost ride my bike without holding on to the handlebars. It's hard and sometimes I fall. I skin my knees all the time. My mom says I'll have scars for the rest of my life for being a kid.

We have a dog. Her name is Gretchen. We used to have Trixie, but she had to go to heaven because she got sick. We have a cat. His name is Frosty. We got him when I was five, for Christmas. Everyone always asks me if he is white because his name is Frosty. He's not white. Frosty is a dark tiger cat with a thick black stripe down his back. We named him after Frosty the Snowman. One time he jumped at my face and bit me. I had to go to the doctor and get a shot. I didn't like Frosty that day; but every other day he sleeps with me at night, and always stays with me when I'm sick. Then he's nice to me.

I love to play with my friends and we play all the time. We run around, play hide and seek, and kick the can, and dodge ball, and softball, and tag, and all kinds of games. It's always fun, especially in the summertime when I get to be outside all day long and I get to run around without my shoes. Well, I'm supposed to wear my shoes, but I don't. I take them off all the time and my mom says she can always tell because my feet are always dirty.

I play the piano and everyone says I'm very good. I don't always need to look at the music to know what keys I have to play. I can hear it and then remember it from my heart. I have to practice every day for thirty minutes and sometimes I pretend that I forget. My mom and dad always remember and I always have to practice. I get nervous when I have to play in front of other people because I don't want to make a mistake.

Last summer, I was playing with my friends and caught a lightning bug. I put him in a jar with some grass and asked my dad to poke holes in the lid so he could breathe. I named him Fred. He got to come and live in the house. My mom said he had to stay in the jar, but I was allowed to keep him by my bed. I got to keep him for a week. Then they said I had to set him free. They said that Fred was really supposed to live outside and not in a jar and it was time to let him go *back to his home. I was really sad when I had to let Fred go. He was my friend.*

On Sundays, we get to play with Dad all afternoon. My mom is in school, too. Not my school, but a school for big people. It's different because she has to practice school when she's not in school and she does that at the church up the street from our house. It's quiet there and we don't get in her way.

Sometimes we do something fun like go for a bike ride or a hike or to the beach; and if we are really good we can sometimes have a treat like Dairy Queen. I like the ice cream cones that get dipped in the chocolate and then the chocolate gets crunchy. How do you think they do that?

When I have a bad dream in the middle of the night, I always call for my dad. He always comes to my room. I tell him about my dream. He always gets me a glass of water and takes me to the bathroom and we check everything just in case anything from my dream is still around. He makes sure it's all gone and puts me back to bed. I'm always able to go back to sleep after my dad chases away my bad dream.

Last summer we went on a car trip to my grandma and grandpa's house in New Jersey. We got to put the seat down all the way and bring our pillows and blankets so we could sleep. I love my grandma and grandpa's house. There is a big door between the kitchen and the dining room and it flaps open and shut. It's just like the doors they have in the restaurant and I like to pretend that we are playing in the kitchen of a fancy restaurant. I spend all day with my grandma in the kitchen and she tells me what to do.

Sometimes we get to go out to the garden way at the back of the yard and pick things. Sometimes we go to the cellar and there is a big freezer where my grandma keeps magic things that she uses when she cooks. She says the freezer helps her make sure she always has what she needs.

My dad told me that my grandpa doesn't hear very well so sometimes I have to talk really loud so he will hear me. People say that my grandpa and I have the same eyes. He always makes me laugh. He doesn't like the crows that fly into the yard and go into his garden. He makes a big scary noise when he sees them to shoo them away. It makes me laugh and when he sees me laugh he always smiles a little. Then he goes back to yelling at the crows.

There was one time I was supposed to be taking a nap and I snuck down the stairs because I wasn't tired and I didn't need a nap. I saw him sleeping on the couch and I tried to sneak past him. All of the sudden, his eyes opened and he looked at me. He pointed his finger at me and then pointed up at the ceiling. It meant I was supposed to go back to my room. Then he smiled and winked and closed his eyes to go back to sleep. I ran up the stairs and jumped into my bed laughing. I love my grandpa.

My hair is short and I don't like it. I had long hair for most of my whole life. It hurt when my mom would try to brush it after it was washed, but I liked having long hair. One night I slept with gum in my mouth. I forgot to take it out. The gum got in my hair. The next day my mom told me that was it.

We went to a hair place and they cut off all my hair. I don't like it. I look like a boy and when people see me and my brother together they think that we are both boys. I'm a girl.

I hide in my closet anytime I think I hear loud voices. There is always a lot of crying and yelling, and it makes me sad because I don't like anyone to be sad. There was one time I heard the word 'divorce'. I'm not really sure what it means but I think it means I wouldn't see my dad. I didn't want that to happen so I ran into the room and said that I wanted to live with my dad always. My dad told me I made my mom sad when I said that. I had to go and say that I was sorry and I did. I didn't mean to make my mom sad.

Christmas was lots of fun and I got a hula hoop from Santa. I don't know how to use it yet. I have a baton already and I know how to jump rope really good, but I can't jump rope in the house, only outside. Last year for Christmas my dad made me my very own cupboard and stove so I could have my own kitchen. I'm a really good cook. At least that's what my dad says. He says my grandma is a good teacher. I'm really excited to stay up until midnight and be awake for the New Year. It's the first time that if I can stay awake, I'm allowed to stay up. We are going to play games and make popcorn.

It's the night before New Year's Eve, and I'm supposed to go to bed early so that I'm ready to stay up for New Year's Eve. I'm in the basement playing when I hear loud voices. I go to the top of the stairs and sit there quietly. It sounds like they are talking about leaving again. I know it's not polite to listen to someone's conversation, but I have to go to bed early and I have to go through the kitchen and that's where they are. I don't want them to know that I'm there and I don't want to get into trouble because maybe they won't let me stay up until midnight for New Year's Eve.

When they leave the kitchen, I run to my room and hide. Later, my dad comes in to say goodnight. He tucks me in. He says, "I love you, Sunshine." I tell him I don't want to go and live somewhere else. He said not to worry and be a good girl always. I fall asleep.

When I'm asleep, I hear a loud noise and it wakes me up. I go to my bedroom door and I hear my mom. I go to find her and she is in the kitchen on the telephone. She is crying. I don't understand what she is saying but something is wrong. I'm scared. I go to my mom and dad's room and my dad is not in the room. I go to my brother's room and wake him up. I tell him something is wrong. He takes me back to my room and we see red lights in the window. We look out the window and there are lots of people in our backyard and there are red lights. We watch.

The garage door is open and the lights are on. Then, I see my dad. He is lying on the ground. He is wearing the blue jacket he wears when he is working outside on a project. He is not moving. I ask what's wrong with Daddy. He doesn't know.

I wait for Daddy to get up. He doesn't. Wake up, Daddy. Something bad is happening. I don't know what it is but it's really bad. Wake up, Daddy. The windows are closed so he can't hear me, but I still keep talking like he can.

Wake up, Daddy. Don't sleep on the ground. It's cold outside. Wake up, Daddy. Then one of the people turns *around and sees my brother and me. They are talking, but we can't hear them. Daddy, you have to wake up. You have to wake up right now. One of them comes into the house and tells us to come with them. He is a stranger in a uniform and I don't want to go. Now I'm screaming, 'PLEASE DADDY, WAKE UP!'*

CHAPTER ONE

Elementary School

My brother and I were taken to the neighbor's house next door while the police processed the scene. At some point, we were brought back home and I remember seeing our family doctor, a police officer, and other adults. My mother told me that my dad had died. There had been an accident and he had gone to heaven. God wanted my dad to be in heaven with Him. I had no idea what all of this meant. I remember a growing sense that whatever had happened was bad. My heart was racing. My mind searched to understand. I slept that night in my parent's bed. I remember making a simple prayer to God. I asked that He make sure that my dad went to heaven.

The next day was New Year's Eve. It seemed as if my mother spent the day in the dining room and kitchen on the phone, making arrangements. The minister from our church was there most of the afternoon. Her brother, my uncle, showed up in the afternoon. That evening, one of the neighbors watched my brother and me at the house while my mother worked on arrangements. We were able to stay up until midnight. We played the board game Monopoly and ate popcorn. I got a big hug from the neighbor at midnight to say *Happy New Year*. I still remember that hug so clearly, mostly because I really needed one. I had no idea what was happening. To this day, I hate New Year's Eve, and Monopoly.

There was a funeral and a memorial service. I was told I had to say goodbye to my dad before they closed the casket. It would be my last chance to tell him good-bye. It was the last time I would ever see him. I could barely see into the casket and I was trying to figure out how to crawl in there with him. I only wanted to wake him up so this nightmare would end and we could go back to the way things were. I was confused when people told me that God wanted my Dad to be with Him. Why would God want my Dad to be with him and not me? What had I done wrong to make him leave?

I couldn't comprehend what was happening. I kept remembering the time I ran into the room when I heard the word divorce. My seven-year old mind, wondered if God was mad at me because I picked my dad over my mother, and now I was being punished. I thought I had done something wrong.

I was told that people were going to ask questions. They would ask us how we were doing. They would say they were sorry. I remember being asked to say that it was horrible accident. It was an awful mistake. He was working on the car, the garage door shut, and he couldn't get out. I was supposed to say, "Thank you, we are fine and we don't need any help". Under no circumstances was I to feel sorry for myself. We needed to be strong and the best thing to do was to try and stop thinking about it. We needed to keep going as if nothing bad had happened. I was confused when I heard that no one wanted to see me cry. This was the first of many times I would be told or reminded that my feelings didn't matter. I learned quickly how to hide my emotions and keep the saddest feelings to myself.

A few weeks later, our dog Gretchen snapped at my brother. Gretchen couldn't stay and I don't recall exactly what happened to her. She was gone in what seemed like an instant and I became fearful of what would happen to me if I did something wrong. Would I be sent away too?

In February, right before Valentines Day, my grandpa died. I remember my grandma said he died of a broken heart, and somehow I understood.

We didn't go to New Jersey for the funeral. I didn't understand what was happening. I didn't know what would happen if I didn't say good-bye to my grandpa. I made a prayer and hoped that he and my dad would be together in heaven. They had each other now and I missed them both.

In my seven-year-old mind, divorce meant your mother and dad lived in different houses. I wondered if my dad was living in another place and dying was just another kind of divorce. I tried to find him when we went out. My plan was I would tell him that I was sorry for whatever made him leave. Every time I came home, I was sad because I didn't find him. I *wanted* him to come home because he was my dad and I loved him. I *needed* him to come home because he was my source of stability and protection. Without him, there was chaos, confusion, and fear.

The summer after my dad died we moved into a townhouse, in a town not too far away. We had a garage sale because we couldn't take everything we had in the house to the townhouse. I was told I couldn't take both the cupboard and stove that my dad had made me. There was only room for one of them. I had to pick which one I wanted to take. I chose the cupboard because I could keep things in it. It broke my heart when someone bought the stove. I didn't cry because I had been told that I wasn't supposed to, but I wanted to badly. My dad had made that stove for me and now some other little girl would be able to play with it.

It was in those first months I recall feeling a more direct influence of my mother's behaviors. It felt as if we were living two different lives. Everything was fine when we went out in public or were around people. She always said how proud she was of my brother and me. I heard her tell people that we were fine and that we could cope with my father's death on our own.

When we were home, it felt different from how we behaved in public. We all felt sadness but in my child's mind, it seemed more vocal and visible from my mother and I experienced it in the forms of sadness and anger. I was mostly afraid I would be sent away because I was bad. I heard that I should be glad my dad wasn't there because he wouldn't know what to do with me. I wanted her to be happy and tried to figure out what would make the crying and anger go away. It seemed important to her that I try to put my father out of my mind and forget about everything. It was then that it seemed to make it better.

I was a kid and I wanted to be a kid, but I felt like I had to make things right, to fix things. I hated when the doors slammed most of all because I was on the other side, alone. There were times the door would fly open a second time, and there would be one more blast of anger or emotion. I would come to wait for that second slam to know that it was over. The loneliness I felt was intense and immense. I don't remember these moments happening every day, but to the seven-year-old girl, the fear it could happen at all was real and seeded deeply within me. I lived in fear that because it had happened once, it could happen again.

My mother finished school and found a job working nights at one of the area hospitals. My brother and I were in the house alone. I was afraid at night and often slept in the trundle bed in my brother's room. Not too long after we moved, the minister from our church started to spend more time at the townhouse, and at some point he moved in. He was going to be our new father. It couldn't have been much more than a year after my dad died. The minister was not a nice man, especially when my mother was not around. It seemed as if he became a monster at night when she was at work. One night, late at night, the minister left. The exact circumstances of his departure are still a little cloudy, except for one thing. I remember being told to say goodbye to him and that I would never see him again. In the first months after he left, I noticed an increase in the frequency and intensity of her sadness and anger.

I was not quite ten years old when the man who would become my stepfather came into our lives. He seemed to like us and he wanted to include us when they went out on dates. It seemed to me that my mother was happy that they were getting married and we were going to be a new family. They were engaged at Christmas and on New Year's Eve, I was allowed to stay up until midnight and enjoy a special treat to celebrate. I was allowed to have my first "grown-up" drink. It was bubbly like soda and made the back of my throat feel almost like it was burning. There were a lot of new people around us. I had new aunts, uncles, and cousins and there was a broader group of adult friends from work and other places. I had been used to social events mostly at the holidays or a birthday, and now it seemed more common for people to make unplanned visits. This made me uncomfortable, and I tried my best to get along and fit in. I was timid and shy, as well as at threshold of the "awkward" preteen years. I was painfully self-conscious. It was new for me to be around alcohol and I recall being offered a sip here and there of something to see if I liked it. It made me nervous to be around people who seemed to change when they drank. I didn't like it when I was the object of attention, especially from the men that were now around more frequently.

From the seven-year-old heart:

I don't know what to do. I woke up. I didn't think I was going to wake up. Or maybe I really died and I'm in heaven and heaven looks just like my bedroom. Except I hate this room. I hate this house, I hate everything. I want my old house and my old room back. And I want my Daddy back. Please.

My head always hurts, it's like someone bumps my head and it hurts, but I don't have a bump and I don't remember bumping it so I don't know how I got the headache. My stomach is always upset. I get sick a lot and have to stay home from school. I'm not pretending to be sick because I love school. School is fun and I'm good at it.

I have bad dreams at night and I'm afraid. It's like I'm dizzy and mixed up and I can't talk and I can't see where I am. I can hear the voices, but I don't always understand what they are saying. Sometimes there is yelling but it's like they are trying to whisper and yell at me at the same time. It smells and tastes gross and I feel like I want to throw up. But I can't throw up because I think throwing up is gross. My whole body hurts and it feels like I can't move or breathe. I don't always remember what happens. I try to block everything out when I remember something because it hurts and I'm scared. If I remember I tell myself that it's not the truth. I try to forget so I don't accidently tell someone. I don't want to mess anything up, so I have to figure out how to not do that. I have to figure this out. Help me figure this out. What do I do?

It would be decades before I recovered any memory of what I have just told you.

CHAPTER TWO

Middle School

The ten-year-old, the protector...

Okay – I'm not sure how we are going to do this, but I'm going to figure it out. I don't want you to be afraid. I'll think of something. I think we need to forget about as much of what happened as we can. This will be my job. No one is going to believe us if we tell the truth anyway. We aren't lying but they are the grown-ups. It's that simple. If I can figure out how to forget about it when it happens, then we won't have to worry about telling by accident and getting into trouble.

I know that you are feeling sad, so let's see if I can try something that will help you feel better. I'm really good at helping you imagine things, so let's play pretend when you are afraid. You can just tell me when something scares you and I'll help you imagine we are somewhere else. When something bad happens, I'll help you get to a safe place, and we will spend some time where you are happy. We won't tell anyone we do this. It will be our secret.

There is another thing we need to do. I think this is very important. We have to be good. We have to be the best we can be at everything. The better we behave, the less likely we are to get into trouble. I'll work hard to get good grades. We won't give them a reason to think we are bad. Let me do this. I'll protect you. I'll take care of us from now on. I promise.

Things will get better at this new house, too. We will be back in our hometown and we have friends there. It will be easier to ride bikes. Our room is bigger. I'll work on those bad dreams. Maybe it won't be as scary, now that Mom will be in the house at nighttime.

You miss Daddy. So do I, but I don't think he's coming back. I think we're stuck with this. I'll work on this, too, and make it feel less sad. Remember how everyone told us after Daddy died that we had to be brave. They said that we were survivors. We had to be strong. I think this is what they meant. That's what we have to do right now. Be brave, be strong, and be good. Survive. And don't tell! I'll figure this out.

My mind blocked and tackled as much of my memory as possible. The sexual abuse gave way to verbal and emotional forms. As I settled into my new life, it seemed as if things changed. The words became meaner and things were said in front of people. It felt to me as if there was an emboldened empowerment that came with the verbal assaults. The power center shifted from sexual and physical to emotional and verbal, yet it impacted me the same. I felt vulnerable about my body as many preteen girls do and it seemed that attention was drawn to my changing body. I was looked at with a wanting leer, except I was too young to understand what that meant. As my memory blanked out, what remained was an undercurrent of fear that I could not shake. My subconscious continued to react to the trauma and yet my conscious mind had lost its perspective. That was the beginning of an inner conflict between my actions, my reactions, and my will.

It seemed I was made the butt of jokes and my presence and the value of my ideas, stories and thoughts were diminished. I was interrupted when I told a story and if I got upset, I was called selfish and spoiled. Conversations often turned to a discussion of rather grotesque experiences related to working with accidents, injuries, and other events common to working in a hospital environment. Graphic, vivid language reinforced the disturbing nature of these incidents and made me very uncomfortable.

Nighttime was the worst. I was haunted in my dreams, terrified. I couldn't remember the details; I could only feel the fear, an overwhelming sense of fear. There was darkness and lots of shadows that moved around me. These shadows took something from me in a violent way. It was as if they were taking away pieces of who I was. I could hear the laughter as they were rummaging through my soul and taking what they wanted from me. I tried to run away, but they found a way to catch me. I saw the eyes - piercing black eyes. I heard level laughter booming as I tried to run. There were occasional variations, but that was the consistent pattern of the terror. I had that same nightmare for decades.

It was during one of those terrors, or waking from one, when I sensed something. I felt it was my dad. When he was alive, I had to wake up from my dreams for him to come and help me. Now, it seemed I could scream for him inside my dream and I could feel him pulling me away from sleep. He was waking me up. He was helping me. I heard his voice telling me to wake up. It seemed as if he was there to rescue me.

The screams were only in my dreams. No one in the house ever heard them and woke up. In those quiet, terror-filled, waking moments my heart raced and it was extremely difficult for me to breathe. I was almost always crying. I steadied myself and listened for my dad. I felt for him, and waited for him to tell me it was all right to go back to sleep. I didn't want anyone to know what I experienced in my dreams. I was afraid that, if I told, it would make it so that my dad wouldn't be able to help with my bad dreams. I needed his help and protection in any way he could give it to me.

We seemed to find a routine as a family. We had moments that were fun. We took summer vacations, had parties and barbeques. My mother's brother, my uncle John, was a steady part of our lives in those years following my dad's death and mother's remarriage. He served an important role in these early years as a safety net of sorts. He was constant and stable and I always felt safe with him. He had a loving, nurturing manner that reminded me of my father. He seemed to like my stepfather, and he kept his interests in my brother and me consistent, even after they were married. My relationship with him was more intellectual in nature and he encouraged me to read, study, and learn.

I went to summer camps. I had friends at school and we did fun things that preteen and young teen girls do. We went to the mall, to the movies, and to the beach. I became interested in clothes and make up and all the trial and errors in finding my "fashion sense" in those awkward years. I became involved in a church youth group. I began babysitting and did it regularly. I loved playing with the children and the quiet freedom that came after I put them to bed and I had the house all to myself. When I was old enough, I obtained a work permit and took a part-time job. Slowly, I started to realize the way out of my fears. It was by staying busy.

I became a voracious reader. I used books to separate myself and create my own space within a room. I worked diligently to never give anyone a reason to get mad at me. I learned how to shut down when an abusive situation presented itself. I learned to divert my focus, and while the abuse was seeping into me, I was taking my mind anywhere else I could. I picked a point and focused on that and allowed my mind to carry me away so that I wouldn't feel the emotions. I got to the point where I could look at someone and pretend I was paying attention to them and what was happening and yet, in reality, I had drifted to a far away, safe space that I had created for myself. I was learning how to block and black out at will.

I hated coming home at night if I had been out with my friends or babysitting. What made me most uncomfortable was the inferred obligation toward the goodnight kiss. It was vastly different from my recollections of saying goodnight to my dad. As I advanced into my early teens, I was old enough to see and understand patterns. I experienced a different tone at night, it seemed somehow more somber and sullen. In the mornings, it seemed more common that I was asked the same questions from the night before as if the conversations were not remembered. I was learning about alcohol and drugs in health class at school. I wondered if it was possible that alcohol was playing a role in the behaviors I was observing and if so, would it be possible to fix it?

One afternoon, I called *Alcoholics Anonymous* from a friend's house and described what I had observed. I was advised to call *Al-Anon.* I called them the next day when I didn't think anyone was home, but someone was there and I was overheard. I tried to explain what was happening. I had figured it out. It could be fixed. I remember a door slamming and the sensation of being alone with my emotions and fears. I was convinced there was no one to protect me and felt no sense of safety. I wept quietly as I wondered why.

The seven-year-old heart...

I thought it was a good idea to call. The people at Al-Anon were really nice and tried to tell me how I could fix things and make it better. I thought I had found a way that I could fix it. I was trying to help. I'm not making things up and I'm not looking for attention. It hurts to hear that I should be happy my dad died because he wouldn't know what to do with me. I don't like it when the door gets slammed and I'm on the other side alone. I'm afraid and I don't think there is anyone here who will protect me. I feel alone all the time.

I had to go downstairs for dinner and I was afraid they would be mad. I walked into the kitchen and sat at the table. I waited for it to happen, for something bad to happen. And then it was so weird. NOTHING happened. It was as if everything was just like dinner last night and the night before. It was as if it had been erased. I ate my dinner as fast as I could and asked to be excused. I couldn't believe it. It was as if it never happened.

Back in my room, it was quiet and I was able to cry some more. I wanted to go somewhere I felt safe. I wanted to be believed. What was happening?

CHAPTER THREE

High School

The ten-year-old protector responds:

Do you see what happens? Are you happy now? I can't believe I let you do this. I listened to you. You told me that we needed to help. You wanted to try and make it better. Do you see where that got you? Look at you. You're a mess. I have been working so hard to get this under control and now, well now, it is exactly as I told you. I told you we wouldn't be believed. I told you to NOT rock the boat. I told you not to make trouble and this was trouble. And you did it anyway. Well, let's just say we both learned a lesson here. Do you see now why you just need to let me fix this and do as I say?

I think I have it almost all figured out. If we keep our grades up, and get involved in as many things as we can, then they will LOVE that we are smart and we like to read and study and learn. It was already working. Try and put this behind you. I wish it had ended differently, but it didn't. We are stuck here.

Do you see what else I have done for us? I know how to put on the face that everything is perfect and that we are a happy family. I can even nod and smile and agree. I'm learning to do that.

I keep blocking out the things we don't like. Now, I'm able do it anytime I need to. You are doing a good job showing me things you want me to make you forget. I'm even figuring out the nightmare thing. Look what happens when we have a bad dream. Daddy comes and helps us. Doesn't that make you feel better? See, he still loves us even from heaven. He loves us so much he comes from there to save us in our bad dreams. I have to say, I'm pretty good at this. I still slip up sometimes, but I'll eventually make this part of us perfect too. I just need a little more time.

Back to my original plan. Do as I say. Don't rock the boat. Stay perfect. I'm smart enough that I'll be able to go to college and I get to go where I want to be. Just stay with me and stop caring about things. You can't fix it. They don't believe us. They never will. Get over it. I'm making it work. Trust me.

After the *Al-Anon* incident, I learned to play by the rules as much as possible so I could maintain the freedom I was gaining. I did not block out what happened that day. My memories prior to this incident were still repressed until decades later. Beginning with the *Al-Anon* incident, and this time forward, my memories are spotty but largely intact.

The high school years were the best of my childhood. I had great friends. It was a small, sleepy lakefront suburb west of the city. The school years were filled with sports, games, and weekend parties. Summers were spent at Huntington Beach and my friends and I sneaked downtown to parties in the part of the city called the Flats. I learned how to manage and escape my life. I was a perfect student. I could keep busy with my job and all my activities and yet I still had time for my friends. I built the perfect façade to keep everyone from knowing the truth. I was quiet, maybe even a bit bookish, and I kept a straight line. I was seeing the payoff. People liked me. They were happy with the work I was doing. Every once in a while I enjoyed a nice conversation with someone's mother. It warmed my heart and made me feel loved.

Things became quieter in the house and we slipped into a routine. It wasn't healthy, but it was consistent and with that there was an odd sense of peace. I had learned how to manage my own emotions, protect myself, and block-out and blackout when I needed to get through a situation. Until my senior prom.

At a pre-prom party, I had a glass of champagne. I either experienced an allergic reaction or somehow the drink had been spiked. I ended up quite sick at the prom and had to leave early. I was sick in my date's car, had chills and I couldn't stop shaking. These continued as I went to bed. I was sick and a bit disoriented, yet have memories of being called a drunk, disgusting, disgraceful, and shameful. I shouldn't think for a minute that my father would know what to do with me and I should be glad he was gone. I heard the door slam. As I lay in bed shivering, I felt destroyed, helpless, and alone. I was exhausted, sick, and beyond tears. I bundled under the covers and tried to stay warm against the chills. I prayed for an end, any end, that could make all of this go away.

The next morning, I explained what had happened to no avail. Because this was prom, I was in deep shit and there would be punishment from school. I would have to figure that one out on my own. If I didn't participate in graduation, I would have to tell my father's mother what I had done.

My guidance counselor happened to be one of my dad's fraternity brothers in college. I made a beeline for his office. I told him everything that had happened and I asked him to tell me the truth. I wanted to know whether he thought that my dad hated me and was disappointed in me for what happened. I remember the warmth of his smile as he gave me assuring words that my father somehow understood and knew that I had made a mistake.

My next port of call was the vice principal. He asked me what happened and I told him the whole story. Everything that I remembered and everything that I didn't remember. I said that I knew I had broken the rules and needed to be punished. I explained that I knew that no matter what decision he made, no one would be able to punish me as badly as I would punish myself. I would carry this for the rest of my life. I was ashamed for my actions. I explained that I was a good student and had never been in trouble before. I had made a mistake and I was very sorry.

He asked me what I thought an appropriate punishment would be. I said that I would go to in-school suspension for as long as he wanted and then that would be it. I would do my time, then have my privileges back, and get to be with my friends for graduation.

He looked at me and then down at his desk as he told me he believed I was sorry and believed my story. I was told to report to in-school-suspension beginning the next morning for five days. I would be able to attend graduation and senior celebrations. As he sent me out of his office to pick up assignments from my teachers, I remember him saying I had made a mistake. We all make them. It's a part of life.

"And Kate?" I looked up and met his eyes. "I accept your apology."

Tears welled up in my eyes. "Thank you." I felt immense gratitude to him, not only because he let it be over, but also because I was looking at the first person that I ever recalled saying they believed me and deliberately accepted my apology.

CHAPTER FOUR

December 21, 1985

My mother's younger brother, my Uncle John, spent a great deal of time with us after my dad died. He became the strong and steady male influence in my life. He was balance, support, and stability. My uncle challenged me, made me think, and helped me focus on education, career, and my future. He worked with me to create a plan for what my life could be. He gave me the light I needed to find a path to my happiness. He gave me hope.

He started law school at the University of Akron the same year I started high school. I admired that at the age of thirty-five, he was willing to take a risk on his future and believe in himself. He was ready to do something big and realize a lifelong dream. He was setting an example for me. He fed my curiosity regarding the study of law. He brought me his old law journals, books, and papers to read. I devoured the readings and immersed myself in the study of law. We sat and discussed what I learned, and he allowed me my questions and opinions. He shared his counter viewpoints. He was the first person to teach me about conversation and perspective. He challenged my opinions and that encouraged me to be more prepared for our next conversation. I believe his intention was to show me how capable I could be at anything I chose. He was the greatest male role model in my life after my dad, and I was very thankful for him.

Kate Elizebeth Nagel

On December 21, 1985 I was home from college on my freshman holiday break. I worked at a small card and stationary shop during high school, and they asked me to come back and help with the holiday season. On that particular morning, the owners asked me to work in their second shop upstairs. I took a call and was asked to go downstairs to the main shop. Julie, the manager, was crying. I asked her what was wrong and then I saw them. My brother and stepfather were in the store. Julie had my things for me and she gave me a big hug. Something was horribly wrong. I kept asking all the way out to the car. They wouldn't tell me. My brother was crying and trying to hide it. My stepfather was stoic.

My brother took the keys to my car and left to go back to the house. My stepfather took me in the other car and told me. My uncle, just hours before that morning, had committed suicide. A shockwave of electric, emotional current forced through my body. It stung my heart, robbed my lungs of air, and surged through every nerve from the core of my soul to the tips of my fingers and toes. I was seven when I last heard similar news, except it was different. I was too young then to understand what death was. I only understood that my dad was gone and not coming back. I was fully aware of the magnitude of death and the now excruciating jolt that came with suicide. I only knew one thing; this was the beginning of something that was never going away. I stared out the car window as we drove back to the house and asked my stepfather some questions in an attempt to get my bearings.

"How?" I asked.

"He shot himself", my stepfather answered.

"Where?"

"In the heart. Twice. He shot himself twice in the heart."

"Was he alone?"

"No, he was with your aunt. Their divorce had finalized a couple days before. It sounded as if they were arguing, but the details are sketchy there."

"How'd he get the gun?"

"It was the same gun from when he owned the bar out at the lake."

"Are you sure? I didn't think he still had that gun."

"Yes, it was that gun."

"Are they sure he shot himself?"

"There will be an autopsy, but the police went to the house he was renting and found notes. Suicide notes. Yes, they feel certain it was suicide."

That was the extent of our conversation. Tears fell down my face in a silent steady flow. I knew I had a precious few moments to release this initial grief and I let myself have what I could. We pulled in the drive and walked into the house. Her face and eyes were swollen and she was catching her breath almost as a child does after an emotional meltdown. A new wave of hysteria started when she saw me. I went to the bathroom and I looked in the mirror briefly thinking, 'this is me, the *child*, once again comforting her, the *adult*.' I grabbed the box of tissues and as I handed her the box, she handed me the wadded soaked tissues in her hands. As I threw those away, I took a couple of deep breaths, pushed back my own tears and emotions, and prepared to support her. I knew there was no comfort for me in this house. I would take care of myself later. It was my job to deal with the emotional chaos in front of me as I had so many times before. Later that night, in the darkness of my room, I cried.

The seven-year-old heart...

Why? Why? Why? Everything was just starting to feel happy and now this. Why didn't you tell me you were so sad? Did you tell me and I didn't hear you? Why didn't I call you on Friday? I wanted to know that you were still coming for Christmas and what time you were going to be here. I'm so sorry that you felt so alone and so sad and that you felt there was no other choice in your life but to die. That must have been so scary. I'm so sorry that I wasn't there for you. I didn't help you. You did so much for me and I couldn't do anything to help you. I didn't know. I'm sorry.

Did you know that you were saving me? Did you know that I wanted to be just like you? Did you hate your life so much that you wanted to end it? I don't know how to be like you right now. I'm so scared; I don't know what I'll be now.

I want to run away. I want to get away, anywhere that's not here. I can't breathe because of everyone else. I'm so sad for my mother, but I'm sad for me, too, and I need to be sad.

How could this happen? How could someone else I loved so much leave me? You were everything I thought I was going to be in my life. I was starting to believe that I could be happy and that I could have all the things I wanted. Why did this have to happen? What do I do now? Who will be here to love me now? How do I do this? What am I going to do?

I'm so sorry. I love you so much. You have no idea how much I'll miss you. I'll miss everything we were going to do together. I'll miss our long talks, the way you made me think, and the way you made me feel strong. I hope you got to heaven and you have peace. I'll miss you. I love you very much.

I cried for hours in the darkness of that first night. I tried to get as much emotion out of me as possible. In the first hours of morning, my perception shifted as the ten-year-old protector stepped up to the plate. She knew it was her job to protect that tender-hearted seven-year-old one more time.

The ten-year-old protector...

Are you okay this morning? How are you feeling? I know you are sad. Even I'm sad too. It's time to start coming to terms with some things. Okay? It's not easy to say this, but I think it's time we know. There are some facts about life I think won't change. First, I don't think that happiness is something we are meant to have. I don't think that people are here to help us. Just look at what happens. We love someone and they leave. We trust someone and they leave. We believe that someone cares about us and maybe they do, but they leave. Daddy, Grandpa, and now Uncle John.

I think it's time to accept that we do not deserve to be happy. We are not good enough for love. We are what they say we are. They must be right when they say that we are no good. I'm going to figure out how we can stop feeling anything anymore. Feeling just hurts us - it hurts you - and it's my job to protect you. I know you are tired. It's been a lot for us and we are only eighteen. We have a long way to go in this life. Let's get through the next few days and I'll figure something out. Just try to stop crying. It will only hurt you more when you realize that they don't care that you're crying.

As the funeral plans came together, the fatigue set in. A deep aching feeling down in my bones. The tired was living deep inside me. I was *eighteen*. I was much too tired for an eighteen-year-old. At the point when my life was just beginning, I began looking forward to the moment I could be done with all these painful things that had happened to me. I wondered whether I could take it anymore. I wondered how I could do this. I wondered how I would live. I had reached a capacity for sadness that I could not comprehend. Yet, it was going to be my challenge now, to figure out how I could push forward in life with all of this.

I had some quiet time to think. The funeral home, the same one we used for my dad's funeral, was in my mother's hometown. It was approximately an hour away on the east side of the city. We drove back and forth between home and Geneva for the visitation and services. I took this time to sort out what it was that I would do. I forced the emotions as far back in me as I could. I stared blankly out the window and listened to the music playing softly in the background. If there was any conversation it came through in a muffled, undetected tone. My eyes were dark from the fatigue, the emotion, and the fear from what could happen next.

The tones of conversation were hushed and any discussion regarding the cause of his death was deflected. During one of the visitations, I saw my great uncle Neal and was a little surprised he was still alive. He walked up to the casket; my mother was standing nearby. He was puzzled and spoke in a very loud voice as if my mother was across the room and not right next to him. "Where did he shoot himself? I didn't think the casket would be open. How did they cover it up? You would never know he shot himself." I smiled a little through some tears as I heard this old man speak the truth.

The funeral was on Christmas Eve. My dad died five days after Christmas. My uncle died four days before. I would never be able to get away from this. The whole world would remind me every year. It's the time of year we celebrate family and love. It is the time of year that we share gifts and take a moment to be grateful for what we have. Every year, it would remind me of all I had lost, all that was lost, and all that I would never know for all that had *been* lost.

Christmas Eve. For the second time in my life and at the age of eighteen, I stood at a casket looking upon a man I loved dearly, trying to find the words, and the way to say good-bye. This time, I was taller and saw clearly into the casket. This time, I was older and stood there by myself. This time, I knew exactly what I was supposed to do.

I stood there and considered the intensity of the word 'goodbye'. I wasn't only saying good-bye to this man. I was saying good-bye to everything; all of my hopes, my dreams and everything I thought possible for me. This wasn't just a goodbye to him; this was a goodbye to me. I made a silent, solemn vow. I'll never let anyone get close to me. I'll figure out how to stop feeling for once and for all. No one has my back, it's just me against the world. This is not about sadness. This is beyond sadness. I'm mad, tired, fed up. I'm not going to let life get me anymore.

And, as I turned and walked out the same door I had eleven years before having said good-bye to my father, I glanced back at the closing casket, and I wondered to myself, when would it be my turn?

PART TWO

The Fortress I Built

The protector…

Okay – here's the deal. I'll fix this.

Let's get some things straight.

First, I know you want to play and laugh, skip and swing. I know you want to be happy. I know you want to believe in all the good things. But let's face it, the days of thinking we could be happy are long gone. They pretty much left the night Daddy died. So what is the point in us thinking that we can be happy? This isn't about being happy. This is about getting through life in the best way we can with what we have.

Second, we are done with feeling sad. You may want to sit there and cry over and over again and have feelings of sadness, loss, and loneliness, but you really need to get over it. No one wants to hear about it anyway, and there is too much work to be done to live this life.

Third, I think it should be abundantly clear to you by now that I need to be in charge, completely and totally in charge.

I'm the brains. I'm the mind. I'm the ego. I'm built to go the distance. You cannot be out in front and we cannot be a team. Look at where that has gotten us up to this point - nowhere good. This is not a democracy. There are no votes. I have all the guts and crass we need to get this done. Trust me. I know what I'm doing.

If you still have any doubt, let me simply say this. I'm an absolute necessity for our survival. I'm our best shot at making it. If you are not on board, we might as well cash it in now. I'll take over how we show up in the world. I'll build all sorts of things that will get us through. I started building these the night Daddy died, and I'll keep going - weapons, shields, masks - all built to protect you. I'll call upon these whenever I feel you are under attack and I'll keep you from harm's way. I'll stay on the ball constantly and revise, retool, recreate, or build anew. Whatever is needed to keep going, make no mistake, I'll take care of us.

If something goes wrong or I think it might go wrong, I'll get out in front and take care of it. Even if I don't know what I'm doing, I'll figure something out. I'll not crack. I'll not break. I can fix anything. Don't worry. I've got this.

You do have one important job. It's up to you to let me know when something hurts, when you are afraid, and when you are sad. I know how to hide all those pesky emotions. Remember what you were told. No one really cares about how you are feeling. Smile, nod, say 'thank you'. Let people know that you are fine. They don't care, they don't want to know, and they aren't going to take care of you. I'm going to take care of you.

I know how to shut down, shout out, and go black. It took a while for me to master this one, and let's face it, there was a lot we had to black out. It was ugly, but it's all good now. If there's something that is just too over the top for you, let me know and I'll take care of it. If there is a crisis, don't worry. I know how to handle it. I know how to completely shut down everything and deal only with getting us through the crisis. Don't worry. I know what I'm doing.

The goal is for you to feel safe; and to live without worrying about all the minor details. You don't need to worry about caring or loving or feeling. These are unnecessary emotions created for the weak. I'm not weak. I'm strong. I'll carry the torch for us and get us through the rest of this life as long as we have it.

I'll build you a beautiful castle so that you may stay safely away from everything that could harm you. I'll create a door so thick and heavy; I'll be the only one to determine when it's all right for it to be opened. I'll build a moat around the castle and fill it with all kinds of things that will eat or kill anything that tries to cross. There will be a massive brick wall that will circle the castle and the moat, and I'll keep building fences and walls as needed.

If anyone dare try to break through uninvited, or challenge this world I have created, then I'll bring the full force of my rage. Let's be clear about this. I know how to get mad. I know rage. But here's the deal. I'm going to do rage better. Not this loud, traumatic, emotional, drama-driven rage. No.

I'll use my mind to formulate a more calculated anger that is measured in tone. It will be based on facts, irrefutable facts. I'll be prepared to defend my opinion, thought, or idea to the end. If it is so, then it is so. There is no need for flexibility because as long as I see it this way, I know it this way, and then I'll be able to defend it. As long as I can defend it, I can win, and as long as I win, you will stay safe. Have you got that?

In the very rare instance where this first approach doesn't work, well then there's Plan B. All I need do is recall a moment of rage from our childhood and I can bring the anger, structure the tone, and pick the words needed to stun our opponent and escape. I can create enough space so that we can safely move away. Abort. Run.

If I happen to hear you in one of these moments, I'll tell you to be quiet. You need not be a party to any of this. You have no need to voice any opinion, thought, or concern. When push comes to shove, this is what I'm built for; I'm made to do this. This is the toughest part of my job and it's best to leave it to the professionals.

You can come out and play only when I'm convinced there is no way you can get hurt. You can play as long as I'm in complete control of everything that is going on around me. If there is the smallest moment when I think you might get hurt, I'll get you back to the castle as quickly as possible. You can count on me. I have your back.

You can count on me because I'm smart. Everything that happened to us taught me how to survive and how to protect you. It is all right to let me take the lead, stay in front, and be in charge. I'm your protector, your ego, and this is my job. I learned everything I need to know to survive. We don't need anyone. All you need is me. Just me.

CHAPTER FIVE

Footings and Foundations

I returned to college a week after my uncle's funeral. I was once again alone with my emotions and I was grateful to be out of that house. I was overwhelmed with grief and sadness. I was frustrated and alone. I was exhausted. I was angry. I readied myself to battle the world. I was in college with the full freedom to act out and rebel. I started framing out the fortress.

I dropped my prelaw major as soon I returned to school. I had to survive and that meant I needed a good job right out of school. I wasn't going to be a lawyer. I was afraid that if I followed my dream of studying the law, it would be only living my uncle's legacy. It would somehow be all about him and all I wanted to do was forget. I wanted something that was mine and only mine. I needed this more than I wanted to follow my passion. My life was now focused on needs, not wants. I walked out of my academic advisor's office and fought away the tears. I was done with crying. I was finished being sad. My life was now about stepping up, bucking up, and making it on my own. It was me and only me.

It's challenging to hide when you are living in a dorm with fifty sorority sisters, roommates, and everyone in your business. In the rare times I messed up or got drunk, it didn't matter as much because it was college and everyone was doing it. To me, it still was not acceptable behavior. Every day, I took steps to lock away the seven-year-old. She needed to feel safe. It was my job as the grown up to deal with it. No more sappy emotions. No more tears. I was done with this. If I was going to have to live in this world, I needed a sustainable world order.

I needed something else to help me figure out how to numb the pain, and the hurts in my life. There were chemical solutions – booze and drugs. I preferred booze. Alcohol had been used as a weapon against me. It was now time to put all that learning to good use, and to turn the weapon used to hurt me into one that would teach me to be stronger. Whereas most use alcohol to escape and avoid, I started using it to create awareness around what I was feeling. It helped me surface the emotions I was working diligently to hide. Drinking allowed the truth to seep out of me. The depressant nature of alcohol helped me get in touch with the emotions – the heart – behind the barriers I was creating. It showed me where additional effort and focus was needed to further learn to hide – block, avoid, and deflect – my emotions. It was a powerful tool for me. I used alcohol to test the tenacity and strength of my protective will against my vulnerable heart. If I was going to do rage better than my mother, then I was going to do drinking better than my stepfather. This was war and I was going to win.

I also built on the practice I started in high school. I got involved and kept busy. I had a part-time job in the admissions office. I was an officer in my sorority; I was President of the Student Senate and served on countless campus committees. I had a day planner by junior year and it was packed with classes, meetings, events, and work during the day and partying at night. Some may have looked cross-ways at the drinking and partying, but you could not mistake my ability to get things done. I was committed and dependable. I delivered results. Keeping busy allowed me to stay on the surface of relationships and interactions with others. If I started to feel as if I was being asked to go deeper into something, I used the excuse of other obligations to avoid intimacy. Busy was my escape hatch. I was afraid to get too close to anyone for fear they would leave. My heart could not withstand another hurt. I rode the surface without dipping my head underwater. It was easier for my heart that way.

It was in those early moments that the workaholic foundation took hold. My "busy" lifestyle was received positively by virtually everyone in my life. I was developing great skills. I was learning how to juggle lots of responsibilities and demonstrating willingness to stretch and grow. I was using work to avoid pain and deflect risk in intimacy and trust. Alcohol was my diagnostic tool and it helped me find weakness within me. Work was my addiction and it helped me hide and avoid. Both were feeding me, fueling me, and allowing me to survive.

The protector...

It's working. See? I told you, it would work. We will become successful in our career, and in business. Life doesn't need to be about who we are, it's about what we can accomplish. It's perfect. No one thinks it's strange. Everyone thinks we are invested in our lives. We are on our way to a very successful life. Everyone says so.

Don't you feel better? You don't have to worry anymore. I'm out in front of this now. I have the formula. I know you get lonely, and you wish it were different. We've talked about this. You've been hurt enough. It's all about what we know, what we can do, and what we can accomplish. Stay with me - keep focused - we are on the right track.

The job market was tight in the late eighties. My first career opportunity blossomed from an internship at one of the largest banks in town. I was accepted into their management training program. I completed undergraduate study with a degree in Business Administration and was fortunate to be one of the few in my graduating class to have a job right out of school. My gratitude further supported the "worker" ethic. It was expected I would feel lucky to have the job and work extremely hard to prove my worth. There would be no summer break for me. I started work less than two weeks after graduation. Work became my source of stability, and my sanctuary. I started to take comfort in the control I could create and maintain in the work environment. I drew emotional satisfaction and self-worth from my efforts and achievements. I could do so with minimal risk and exposure to my heart.

The organization was in a high growth mode. I became part of a team that worked on merger and acquisition deals and in short time, came to have greater responsibility in this process. It was high pressure, intense, and deadline-driven. It was highly confidential work most of the time, and that meant I couldn't talk about it. I loved it. I accepted every assignment offered. I stayed late, worked weekends, and did whatever was needed to get the job done. I juggled multiple assignments and I always seemed to make a deadline. I was described as "high strung, in a laid back kind of way." Managers told me it was the best way to describe someone with an insatiable appetite for work that was balanced by a good-natured willingness to do whatever was needed to help. I seemed to take it all in stride.

I became quite good with change management. I knew how to work within, and, more importantly around, a system to get the results that management wanted. I lacked the emotionality that got in the way of difficult decisions and choices. If there was a tough call to be made, ask me. I'd make it.

Working relationships could be personal, but they weren't always intimate. I could know a lot about the people I worked with, I could trust them, but there was always a boundary and line that I didn't need to cross. I didn't need to go to that "emotional" place. It was perfect because

I didn't know *how* to go there. I had the interpersonal connection we need as humans without the depth or requirement for intimacy and deep trust that comes with a more personal relationship. I had a life outside of work with friends and boyfriends, but I didn't know how to dive deeply into the essence of them or me. I was afraid to try because going *there* meant *they* would leave and *it* would hurt. I had a long, painful history backing me here. Every time I thought about it, I couldn't.

I developed this ability to get to know people, to talk a lot about me, but not say a lot about me. I kept my cards close to the vest. It was only on a very rare occasion that I allowed someone through the barriers. It was usually after they worked diligently and intently to tear through them and convince me that they were not going to hurt me. I could skim the surface and it would be enough to keep me going. This was the birth of the inner conflict between the two – my seven-year-old heart and my ten-year-old protector - the heart that wanted to live and love and the protective ego that wanted to avoid it and enjoy the rush that came from work.

After two years, routine settled in. I was finding more time on my hands and was ready for another challenge. The bank had a tuition reimbursement program. I was accepted into an MBA program at the same school where I completed my undergraduate work. It was a two-year program and I worked full-time and attended graduate school full-time. My life revolved around work and school for the next two years. I built within myself an even higher capacity for work. I could sustain eighty-hour work and school weeks for months on-end. There were moments when someone might ask me if I was doing too much, and working too hard. I shrugged this off and said that if I wanted to get ahead and get to a place where I didn't have to work quite as much, then I had to pay my dues now. I was focused on a professional track. I had created a protective façade to support the life that I was equipped to live. My life was based on work and not personal. Facts, not feelings. Achievements, not emotions.

And, with every hour logged, every meeting, every class, every project, every job title, every degree; my protective, ego-driven persona became stronger, more capable, and fully in charge. The workaholic advanced, and the heart retreated. As I checked off every box on the list of what I thought I needed in my life, I just kept adding to it, convinced that at some point I would have checked off enough things and my life would be exactly what I needed. And the seven-year-old girl, the heart of my soul, was tucked safely away behind walls built by the protector. The fortress was complete and ready for any battle. Every now and again I would hear her, I would see her peek out and wonder if it was all right to play. The answer was always, "No. Stay in there. Don't come out. You will only get hurt. Let me keep going. I've got this."

CHAPTER SIX

Framing and Finishes

About six months after finishing graduate school, I was recruited to work for a small consulting firm in Washington, D.C. I was leaving the town I grew up in and starting a new life on my own. I found my escape hatch. I moved into an apartment in North Arlington, rode the Metro to work, and enjoyed the feeling of living in a big city. I was ready to take my career to the next level. There are some who believe that consulting allows you to accumulate an extraordinary amount of experience in a short of period time. Some say as many as three years for every year worked. I was eager to accelerate that process and learn as much as I could. I came to D.C ready to work.

Consulting gaslit the workaholic addiction within me. I was sparked before I even started. I planned to take a couple weeks off between jobs. I needed to physically move from Ohio to D.C. and then wanted to take a little time and explore the city. I was asked to start early so that I could go on a client assignment that would orient me to consulting. I should have felt angry, but I was thrilled. On my first day of work, a week earlier than I had anticipated, I arrived in the office with my garment bag in tow, ready to hit the ground running. That first day launched what became a nonstop work frenzy that spanned almost two years.

Consultants are fixers, and in this I found a career that allowed me to live into something I had been practicing since childhood - making everyone happy. The concept was to solve the problem before it becomes one, and if it becomes one, I fix it as quickly as possible before anyone finds out. I was being paid to do something that was inherent and instinctive to me. If there was problem at-hand, give it to me, and I would take care of it. I could see forward into a process, figure out what could go wrong, jump in and save the day. I was good at it.

Consultants give advice, opinions, and tell you what they would do if they were you. I was good at that. I had learned how to compile data in support of analyses and construct conclusions and recommendations. My favorite part of the process was the moment someone challenged my analysis. That allowed me to access and develop my ability to argue and defend my opinion. All I needed to hear was that someone questioned the accuracy or the underlying methodology of the analysis and I was off and running. Defense of analytics fed my inherent need to be believed. Whether I would be *right* straight away or *right* after debate and discussion, I was always *right*. The feeling I got in those moments when someone affirmed my work or recommendation fed my need. My craving for this feeling intensified. There were many times when I heard that I would have made a great attorney. People asked me whether I had I ever considered the law as a career.

I was a great facilitator and even early in my career, I was "sent in" to the room to guide executive teams to decisions. I knew how to show up as expected. I walked in, read the temperament and energy, found the "dark spots" of anger and resentment, and then adapted myself to win the favor of the resentful and make sure that I landed exactly where the client wanted. Show up, be good, get along, and maintain the illusion that I am exactly what they think I am. Stick the landing.

The billable hours model in consulting fueled my capacity for work perfectly. I had weeks when I billed up to ninety hours and was on the road all week. I would be out on Sunday, back on Thursday, having spent days in front of clients, nights working on analyses and presentations, and time in between moving in and out of airports. I worked all weekend to get ready to go back out on the road. My closet was organized into three-week rotations of clothes ready to be packed for travel. I packed Week One, travel, dropped it at cleaning on Saturday and then packed Week Two. Week Three was my back up, in case I didn't have a chance to stop at the cleaners when I was in town.

I knew the woman at the dry cleaner by her first name. She got my things without needing my ticket and she repaired any button, zipper or hem without my asking her to. Travel went on like this for weeks at a time. If I had a week in the office, I worked late every night and after a day or two, I had the itch to get out on the road. I knew the desk guard in the office building who walked me to my car most nights, and the driver that took me to and from the airport. I knew more about this woman and these men than the neighbors in my apartment building or the guy whom I was currently dating.

One January, I was sick with a sinus and respiratory infection. It was the result of traveling, airplanes, hotels, and non-stop work. While on a flight to visit a client, I experienced significant pain in my ears. On the flight home, this problem worsened and my right eardrum "blew." I couldn't hear. I was sitting next to the Managing Partner and he was talking. I told him to stop being funny, and talk so I could hear him. He was, and I couldn't.

The next morning, I woke up to find that I had missed my alarm all together as well as three calls from the office. They had arranged for me to see an ear, nose and throat specialist that afternoon, before I had even asked. I went into the office to take care of some things, and then I went to the doctor. I was at a ninety percent hearing loss in my right ear and forty percent in my left. The doctor grounded me for six weeks from air travel and sent me to bed for three days. The doctor felt my hearing would restore when the infection and inflammation cleared, but there was permanent impact from this. When the infection cleared, I ended up with a twenty percent hearing loss in my right ear. I kept going.

One Friday afternoon, I was sitting in a meeting and someone said that I needed to leave. My face had swollen up on the right side. Was I in pain? I said I had noticed some pain in my mouth, as a wisdom tooth had been trying to break through. It had been bothering me, but I did not feel it was a big deal. I walked into my dentist's office, conveniently right up the street. I was rushed upstairs to the oral surgeon's office. He was shocked by the severity of the situation and said I should have been in a lot of pain. Twenty minutes later, my severely infected, impacted wisdom tooth (that was growing in sideways) was pulled out. I stopped back in the office, antibiotics and pain medications in hand. I had to clean up a couple of things before I left for the day. It would be a couple of hours before the anesthetic wore off. I kept going.

I had a few conversations with people who expressed concern about my well-being and work driven lifestyle. Yet no one considered it an addiction or something negative. I was hard working and driven. I was putting in my time in order to accelerate, achieve, and grow. I had an enormous capacity for work. I always had, and I felt that I might as well use it now to take me where I wanted to go, except I had no idea where I was going. I only knew work was my escape from everything I didn't want to face.

I was working non-stop and taking any assignment that was offered me. My first year, I billed my annual quota in the first six months. It was a high stress, intense working cycle. We worked from project deliverable to deliverable, always being on time, always being perfect. Much of my work relied upon information to be provided in a timely fashion and technology to work efficiently. This didn't happen often. If a client was late getting us information we needed for a presentation, that was our problem, not theirs. We were still on the hook for our deadline. This often meant working at a breakneck pace to make sure we were always on time and always right. I sunk deeper into my addiction and it became darker. I became darker.

My nerves became raw, my patience wore thin, and my tolerance dropped to zero. My interactions with colleagues became harsh and abrasive. I became less concerned with my interpersonal behavior in favor of the manic flow of work, perfection and performance. The demand for my time on projects was high and I was generating substantial revenue for the firm. The leadership team seemed pleased with my contributions and perhaps overlooked my behaviors in favor of the bottom line. I assured them I was fine. I had no boundary for work. It's all I did. I started to expect the same thing from others. If I was prepared to stay all night, then why couldn't they? It was a deadline-driven world and that meant late nights, weekends, and sacrificing personal life. It's what we'd signed up to do. It was the price of experience. If that didn't happen, the work became my "burden" and I took it on myself, sometimes "saving the day." I had no ability to set reasonable expectations for myself or others. My first priority was to always to get the work done; everything else was secondary in my life. My managers and clients loved it. My colleagues did not agree.

The pressure I placed upon myself to be perfect and right, under these conditions was extreme. The margin for error was zero. I ran in a full sprint toward deadlines. There was a high I felt when I hit a deadline and there was an extra kick when the client was happy. Afterwards, there was a "crash," much like the lull experienced after an adrenaline or sugar rush. This lull left me searching for the next high. I kept three or four project deadlines going at any one given time, in order to stay on the high. I did anything to avoid the crash. Work was my drug and I kept in constant search for my next hit. I did anything to avoid the possibility of a crash.

I was twenty-eight years old and spinning on all cylinders. I had been on this course since graduate school – maybe even high school and college. It was impossible for me to do anything other than work. I rarely took personal time off and even I when I did, I created situations and opportunities to work. Even before the Blackberry ®, I stayed as "plugged in" to the workplace from wherever I was. It consumed me. I slowly began to find myself in a tired state that I couldn't shake. I woke up in the early hours of the morning and looked at my darkened eyes and ashen face and couldn't remember when I had been in the sun last. I felt like I kept getting pulled underwater, let up for air for a minute, and then was pulled back under until I almost passed out. I didn't know how to change it. I spun like this in a downward spiral for nearly two years until the day I hit rock bottom. I was doubled over with pain and collapsed in my office.

CHAPTER SEVEN

The Hidden Cost of Building

In the midst of my D.C. working frenzy, at the height of my addiction, I experienced my first major crash. I was twenty-eight. There had been something physically wrong with me for years. I had always had a lot of pain with my menstrual periods and it had been worsening since I had moved to Washington D.C.. Doctors had assured me repeatedly that this pain was not uncommon, and it would likely clear up when I had children. Until then, I would have to tolerate it. I was given multiple painkillers like Percocet®, to manage the pain. I used the medications when it was debilitating but the pills left me sluggish and disorientated. I couldn't miss work, and I taught myself how to ignore the pain as best as I could, so that I could keep working.

My assistant found me on the floor. I was conscious, but crying and unable to move. Two phone calls later and I was on my way to see one of the top gynecologists in Washington D.C. She was seeing me as a favor to one of the Managing Partners. The ultrasound showed a substantial mass in my right pelvic region. I needed surgery. She wouldn't rule out cancer. I would be out of work for approximately eight weeks and it might be longer before I would be able to travel.

A good friend of mine was a radiologist. He looked at my films and he asked me whether I was in pain. I said that I was sometimes. He said, "Kate, you should be in a lot of pain, all the time." I asked if he thought it was cancer. He said that he didn't think it was, but he couldn't be certain. I asked him why he thought that it wasn't. He said simply, "If this is cancer, I'm pretty sure you would be dead, or very close to it."

I phoned my mother and she became quite emotional upon hearing the news. I heard her sob that she didn't know what she was going to do if this was cancer. She wouldn't know what to do if she lost me. I sat there and thought, "What are *you* going to do if it's cancer?" I sat on the other end of the phone in disbelief. I was not sure if I had cancer, if I was going to live or die, or what was going to happen to me. What seemed to be important to my mother in that moment were *her* feelings about the possibility I might be dying.

She insisted that she come stay with me after the surgery. "Absolutely not" was my first thought. The last thing I needed was to have my mother there while I was trying to recuperate from major surgery. I would be trying to heal and it would be all about her. I told her politely that I appreciated her offer to help, but I was fine. One of my sorority sisters from college was living in D.C. and she agreed to stay with me. My radiologist friend lived on the other side of the courtyard. I had plenty of friends to help me with things while I was getting better. I had this all under control. The doctor told me that all I would want to do was sleep the first few days. I would be fine.

The surgery followed a few weeks later. The diagnosis was endometriosis.[1] I wasn't dying. It wasn't cancer. It was an autoimmune disease, and one of the worst cases my doctor had ever encountered. It required aggressive treatment, and there were things she couldn't fix. This diagnosis was not the end of the situation. It was only the beginning.

I was back in her office about a week later. The first thing she wanted to know was how I had been functioning. The pain should have been extreme, intense, and debilitating. She asked how I was able to block out such intense physical pain. I responded simply, "You have no idea what I'm capable of blocking out. I was told this was something I would have to deal with it, and that's what I did." She was more than concerned. Physical pain is an indication of the disease, and my thresholds were extreme. I needed to be conscious of my pain. What had I heard? I had to acknowledge, define, and address pain as an ongoing, inevitable part of my life. If I wanted to restore and maintain my health, there would be no more blocking it out. I looked at her and uttered a single word under my breath. Shit.

The next thing she told me was this endometriosis was a chronic disease. It may go into remission, and it could stay in remission for years, even the rest of my life, but it was a disease. There was no control over its pattern or progression. It had all of the power in choice to thrive or diminish. It was in charge. I had to go where it took me. We could manage it as best as we could, but there were no promises. There were lifestyle choices I could make that may help as well. I asked her what choices she meant. She looked at me, raised an eyebrow in a motherly way and smiled a little, telling me that respected researchers had found a direct correlation between stress and the progression of the disease. The more stress you put on your body, the greater the likelihood for progression. Here's what I heard: I couldn't control this. I couldn't block it out of my life. I couldn't fix it. I needed to slow down. Shit.

She mentioned a considerable amount of scar tissue and damage. She questioned whether I had been sexually abused as a child. I had remembered emotional and verbal abuse, but I had no recollection of sexual abuse. I told her there was a period of roughly eight years in my childhood that I couldn't remember. She was the first doctor I had told about my repressed memories.

It was time for the tough news. I braced. Because of the extent of the damage and the severity of the disease, it was virtually impossible that I would ever be able to have my own children. It would be a significant, uphill battle. The older I got, the less feasible it would be. I still had one ovary, but the statistics were not with me. Further, if I were able to conceive, the likelihood was low that I would be successful in carrying a baby to term. The odds were not on my side. She wanted to be as honest as she could be with me. We would do everything we could and would be aggressive, but the damage was severe. She was sorry.

Here's what I heard: You can't fix this. You can't be fixed. You are broken. You broke yourself. And then, I heard a small voice from deep within. It came with some tears and disbelief,

NO – why is this happening?

She gave me a hug as I left. For the moment, I needed rest, lots of rest. I needed to keep my stress levels as low as possible. She told me that if I had any pain that was bad I should call the office or the after hours service, and I should not ignore the pain. I should read a book, take naps, sit outside, get some fresh air, and relax. It was important that I minimize my stress levels in every way I could and that meant absolutely no work. I left her office in a bewildered state. I went home, crawled into bed, and spent the rest of the day in a state of shock. My mind didn't know how to process all I had heard and my heart crumbled as it struggled with the questions of how and why.

The next morning, I attempted to get a handle on things. I made some breakfast and took a short walk. I was moving better and the fresh air did my spinning head some good. I thought I was making some progress. I came home, made some tea, turned on the television, and found a newsbreak had interrupted regular programming. There had been an explosion at a government building in Oklahoma City. It was April 19,

1995. I sat there and watched the events unfold and was horrified to learn there was a daycare center in the building. The loss of life included young children, babies. I watched mothers looking frantically for their children. The emotions showed on their faces. I considered the excruciating pain and grief that would come with not knowing where their children were and if they were safe. I couldn't fathom the unimaginable, devastating reality some would face if they learned their child was injured or had not survived.

I sat there immobile, riveted, and despondent. I broke down. This was the first time I was not able to control my thoughts or emotions. I cried in a way I don't think I had ever cried before. With each heaving sob I could feel the pull from my incision. Each deep, sobbing breath was filled with physical pain and even more emotional pain. I cried for every mother who had a child there that day. I cried for their pain, their terror, that pure, unconditional love they may never get to show their children again. I watched them searching. I watched them reeling with pain, terror, and fear. In that moment, my heart unleashed. It had been locked up for almost two decades. My soul walked right up to my ego, punched her in the face, and told her to shut up. Stop it. Stop it right now. Let my heart feel.

> *... and my seven-year-old heart just cried out in pain and sorrow*

> *Look at what's happened. Those mothers are looking for their children. There are missing, hurt, and dead babies. What are those mothers going to do if they lost their babies, and their children? What will I do? What am I going to do? Why did this happen to me? I'll never get to know them. I know they are out there somewhere and I'll never know them. This is all your fault.*

How could I let you do this to me? How could I let you be in charge this long? This is too much. How did you ignore everything? You told me to trust you. We were hurting and now there's nothing we can do. It's over before it even started. You told me to trust you. You would fix everything. Well, you fixed this good. Who will want to be with us now? You broke us. You worked so hard you broke us and now there is no way to fix us. What are you going to do?

Never mind, I don't want to talk to you right now. Go away. I just want to rest. I want to be quiet. I want to be sad for those mothers. I want to be sad for me. Just sit there and shut up and let me cry as long as I want. I have followed your rules long enough. We aren't supposed to work anyway. I get to do what I want for a little while.

I had no mechanism within me to avoid or manage these emotions. My heart ached and I gave in. I let it wash over me. I let it consume me. I didn't try to fight it. I couldn't fight it. I didn't know how. I cried until I passed out and then awoke hours later and started again. It went on like that for days. I just couldn't stop. People checked in and I collected myself enough to get through the visit or conversation. I shared some of the realties of diagnosis. I needed to lower my stress levels; I needed to consider making some changes in my life. I didn't tell anyone that I wouldn't be able to have children. I couldn't bring myself to say it out loud. I was ashamed.

Something changed in me that day. Oklahoma City. I discovered an unexpected, exorbitant price to my non-stop, relentless working habit. A crack formed in that well-sealed barrier of my fortress. I spent my last weeks of recovery outside in the sun as much as possible. I walked and read. Springtime in D.C. was lovely. I didn't miss work and this surprised me. I wasn't looking forward to using work to shield my heart from this devastating situation. I was confused and heartbroken. My medical leave dwindled, and I knew it was time to pack up my emotions as much as possible. It was time to formulate a plan, to figure out what I would do next.

The protector...

Are you feeling better? I let you have all this time to be out and get rid of your hurt. I'm sorry that this happened. I didn't think something like this could happen. I'll figure out how to fix things the best I can. I don't want you to be sad, or angry. You are supposed to be safe and happy. I'll start to think some things that we can do differently that will make it a little easier on us.

Maybe this happened because we weren't supposed to be a mom. I know you wanted the chance to be a better Mom than our Mom, but I don't think it's supposed to happen. It's just not something we were built to do. We are built to work. We probably don't have much of a shot of what you hoped for. The husband, children, home. The happy life you wanted.

Work is what we have now. We have to keep that going. We can try to get the other things you want. Maybe we should move somewhere else. We could make a fresh start. Maybe we can find someone who will love us even though we are broken. I don't want you to get your hopes up though. It may be time to get out of here.

I started back to work slowly and built up to a full schedule during the next couple of months. My colleagues were considerate and limiting to my travel schedule for as long as possible. I started to feel their anxiousness. They were waiting to see when I would "come back" and be the power biller I had been. I recalled a Managing Partner saying in one meeting, 'If you were able to bill at almost twice your capacity, what are you capable of now that you are actually healthy?' It was a good question, a terrifying question. I caught myself and I didn't want to know the answer. I knew then that I was finished there. It was time to cut and run.

Having lunch one day with a friend, I told her I was considering a career shift. She thought I might like the company where she worked. I had used their products for years. It would be a good fit. She would connect me with the Group President. The working sales culture there was less intense than my current consulting environment. She had a great life. She worked long hours and traveled, but had balance. She was able to have a personal life, travel, and have lots of fun. It sounded like exactly what I wanted. I told her I wanted to get out of Washington D.C.. This would be no problem as they had offices across the country. In fact, she was moving to Chicago.

CHAPTER EIGHT

The Foundation Cracks

Chicago. Now that sounded interesting. It had all the life of a big city nestled in the heart of the Midwest. I thought that the people might be friendlier and somehow feel more familiar. I met the hiring executive for drinks one night and he offered me a job. There was a strategic vision to evolve and transition the sales team to become more consultative and pursue service-based revenue. Chicago was a great place to centralize this new strategic vision and I personified it perfectly.

It was a new business model and Chicago was a great launchpad. It might be viewed as a big change. It's possible the change would shake things up and it might shake some people out. Was I up to the challenge? Absolutely. I knew consulting was a burnout business and I was beaten and worn by it. I was convinced it was the job, the company, the profession that had caused me to be the way I was. If I changed that, I would be fine. I needed a break. The frenetic pace I had chosen to operate at for years had beaten me down, but I wasn't ready to admit it. I was blaming everything on external conditions. I was being offered a chance to start a new chapter of my life. I was going to take that job and move to Chicago. I would wipe the slate clean, as if it had never happened at all.

The offer arrived and I jumped at it. I flew to Chicago to meet the team. I was blindsided by the first difficult issue. They had no idea I was coming. They had no idea I had been hired to work for the company, let alone that I was coming to work in Chicago. I was the number two behind the Regional Vice President. I was taking a senior position and that meant that I was automatically assigned to an office with a door and a window view of Michigan Avenue. In doing this, and unbeknownst to me, I bumped off someone on the team who had been with the company a long time, and was next in line for an office with a window. My position was senior to her and I took her slot. Guess who was not going to be asking me to lunch anytime soon?

I told myself that I had survived far more complex and uncomfortable situations. We were all professionals and this was business. I had a job to do to bring change to the company. I would get that done. I needed to get that done. Once the strategic vision became clear, it seemed as if battle lines were drawn. I was advised that no one liked me, no one there would make it easy for me, and no one there wanted me there. There was resentment of me coming and being tasked to tell them how to do implement this new strategic idea.

It was clear to me. I was stuck. I could defy the corporate goal and risk being fired. I could defy the regional team and risk further escalation of their apparent dislike of what I represented. I tried to tell myself that they didn't hate me, they simply hated the agenda. I wasn't doing anything wrong.

I dug in my heels, and stepped up to the challenge. I was desperate to make this work. I hadn't taken time off between the jobs nor had I spent any time recovering from the D.C. consulting burnout, my surgery, and my inability to have children. I just plowed forward. This was my price to pay for my new life. I wanted a life in Chicago. This was my best shot at the "happy" the heart wanted. It had to work out. My health needed this to work. My heart wanted them to like me. I tried to rally to fight this battle. They may win the fight, but I would win the war. I knew how to win wars.

There was something with respect to this situation that I couldn't connect until almost twenty years later, as I wrote this book. I wondered why I was feeling this sense of fear and danger when I was in the office. There was a woman on our team that caused me to have a visceral reaction. I "took" her office when I started there, and I sensed strongly she didn't like me. I couldn't understand why I was unable to shake the feeling of having to defend myself. I was agitated anytime we were both in the office. It was fine when she was out on travel. In fact I felt relief. She had dark brown hair and piercing eyes. She had the same long lashes, the same color, and everything. It was as if I was looking at a vision of my dark and frightening past every day.

However, I couldn't make the connection between these points because I was repressing the memory. My subconscious mind was triggering a safety, avoidance, abort reaction, and my conscious mind had no idea why this was happening. It was deep, inner conflict with my memory and it was beyond my capacity of awareness. I thought this battle was regarding work, but it wasn't. This was a dark corner of my soul being illuminated. It was like my soul was trying to get me to remember something I didn't know I needed to know.

When I was in the office, I experienced it as a junior high, "you don't belong" kind of mean. There were jabs, jibes, and subtle cruelty. I heard them talk behind my back. They made plans in front of me and not include me. If I asked for help with something, I sensed great resistance. The personal feelings that I had worked for years to bury, were hurt. I couldn't believe that behavior was happening in the workplace. Every day I felt like a bullied, displaced kid on the playground. I was doing my job. It was business.

I started to look in the mirror and see what I think they saw. I was guarded and nervous around them. I was forcing the corporate agenda for change at every opportunity. I tried to instill the consultant's "get it done" mentality. I was reluctant and afraid to open up personally. I was uncomfortable and defensive in most situations, as if I was preparing for an assault. They didn't know why I was this way. Maybe what they were saying was true. Maybe all the things I heard growing up were true. I began to wonder what was happening to me. I had changed everything – job, city, life. I began to consider the cause of my unhappiness. I was once again, within months, completely miserable and burnt out. What I had failed to recognize was the common denominator in all of this. Me. I was the one that had created this. I was this broken self. My will was giving way. The years of being a workaholic were bearing down upon me. What had gotten me to a place of great success in my career, was backfiring on me. I was tired, so very tired. I hit rock bottom.

I stared straight in the mirror and saw everything I was, everything I wasn't, and everything I was not capable of being. I couldn't argue with them. I didn't like me either. I hated myself for who I was. I started to buckle. I started to lose my fight. I couldn't fix this. I was failing. Oh - I did not like to fail. I didn't know what to do.

I was running on empty. The bathroom in my apartment was a shade of gray. I remember thinking it an odd color choice. Now, when I looked at the mirror, I couldn't see me but for the walls. I was fading, dissipating into the paint and the walls. I was fading away to nothing.

A depression started to sink in. It was a layer of exhaustion I had not known before. I was exhausted from the travel, exhausted from the work, exhausted from being alive. It kept me from getting out of bed in the morning and sent me to bed almost as soon as I got home from work every night. I hardly ate. When I was in bed, I couldn't sleep, but I couldn't get up, either. I didn't care if there were dishes in the sink or if

I remembered to take the trash out. I stopped caring about everything, because nothing mattered anymore.

The next layer sunk in. I stopped being able to feel anything. I went numb. I was affected by everything that I stopped being affected by anything. I wasn't capable of processing. It was a state of emptiness I had never known. I had no ability to figure out how to make it go away. There was a part of me that didn't want to. Maybe this was what I deserved. I wasn't meant to be happy.

I couldn't make this go away. Too much had happened, and my ability to block it out had given way. Something opened in me that the day in the doctor's office after my surgery. Oklahoma City. Some portal in my soul opened up and my mind hadn't shut it down properly. It was a small crack in the foundation of the fortress. The crack was continuing to spider out and fragment, allowing emotion and feeling to come forward, and I was not equipped to deal with it. I had no ability to work with emotion, only to bury it.

I thought of the conversation when I was hired. I was presented the opportunity to influence change within an organization as something like a Darwinian experiment - survival of the fittest. Who would adapt, and at the same time accepting that some might fall away and leave. It became clear to me that I was not going to survive. I would fail the Darwinian experiment. I was officially broken. It seemed the one thing I thought I could have, that of a career, was slipping away. I was losing hold of the one thing I had - work.

I cried all the time. In the morning before work, walking to work, walking home from work, and in bed before I went to sleep in the dark. I stayed in the dark as much as possible. I didn't like the light. It hurt my eyes. I wanted to stay in the dark. There wasn't a single breaking point, but rather a series of events over time and a very slow, painful breakdown.

Life was telling me something, and I started listening. It had been eleven years since my uncle's funeral and the question I wondered as I said goodbye to him. I didn't know if the day would ever come, but now it was upon me.

It was my turn.

The gray turned quickly to black and it started to seep in. The darkness became blacker than anything I had ever seen before. It was everywhere. Even when I knew it was day, it was night. It was black. It never changed and just when I thought it wasn't possible to get any darker, it got darker. It became a new shade of black, darker than anything I had ever seen before, and it spiraled down like this. I don't know if it changed every week, every day, every hour, every minute. It just kept getting more and more black, and I didn't know how to make it stop. I didn't want it to stop. There was a disturbing comfort that came with darkness. It was easier to live in the dark and believe all of the bad things about me, then to fight my way to light.

The air around me was thick and murky with an almost sludge-like feeling to it. It was like I was breathing in soot. It weighed down my lungs to the point where simple breathing was an effort. Each inhale introduced another thin layer of gunk. Every exhale did nothing. There was no release, no expelling the poison, and I continued to take it in.

The sound around me became muffled, like I was underwater. I couldn't hear what people were saying to me. They talked. I nodded. I made comments, but I wasn't listening. I wasn't participating. And I forgot as soon as someone said something. I didn't need to retain any more information. It was my turn after all, and I felt there was nothing left to learn. I felt as if I was on a boat sailing in the middle of nowhere in this thick black sea. Someone was screaming at me to take the wheel, to steer me away, but I couldn't hear. The wind or the waves were making a lot of noise and it drowned out the voices.

The downward spiral felt fast in a slow motion kind of sensation. I could see myself, but it was almost an out-of-body experience. It was not a good one. I watched myself with a morbid sense of fascination as I plummeted down a narrow, steep ravine. I knew there was the moment I would hit. I didn't know when. I knew it would be intense for a moment. The energy force compelling the plummet was immense. It might be cold and dark and scary when I hit, but it wouldn't last long. If I had done it correctly, it should end quickly.

I didn't know exactly how to do this. I quietly started to get things in order. I planned what would go where, who would need to know what, and how much things might cost to make sure I could take care of it all. I didn't want anyone to suffer because of me. Even as I contemplated the end of my life, I needed to be sure I had taken care of everything. My uncle consumed my thoughts, how he had planned it out, and how much time and thought had he put into it. There would be notes. I started working on those. I didn't know exactly when or how. All I knew was that it was my time.

One night not too long after I had come to this conclusion, my friends dragged me to a Chicago Cubs game. I didn't want to go. They told me I had no choice. I needed to get out. It was a beautiful night, a perfect night to be in the ballpark. I gave into their demand. I love baseball and if this was my last, at least it was a Cubs game. It was actually a nice distraction and I settled into the rhythm and strategy of the game. It calmed me a bit. After, we went to a bar called Sluggers. It had batting cages upstairs. I was sitting at a table by myself while my friends were in the cages. I was up next. I was drinking a beer when a guy walked up to me.

He said, "You seem sad." I looked at him with no expression and replied, "Yes, I'm sad." He reached into his pocket and handed me a gold token.

He said, "Here, take this." It was a token from Sluggers and it had the date 8/8/88 and the phrase "I saw the lights" on one side.

I said, "Thank you" and I looked at the coin. He kept talking.

He said, "You know, they swore they would never play a night game at Wrigley Field. They would never light that field. There was a lot of effort to keep it dark. But you know something? The world keeps changing, and somehow the impossible becomes possible. The lights come on so you can see and play in the dark. Remember that always. Okay? Promise me."

I kept staring at the coin and my eyes welled with tears. I said, "Okay, I will." I looked up, and he was gone. I looked all around and he was nowhere to be found. I went up to my friends and asked them if they saw the guy I was talking to and where he had gone. They looked at me as if I was crazy. They held out the bat for me. It was my turn to step into the batting cages and take a swing.

I looked at the coin in my hand. I looked at my friends. I had to go. I ran downstairs, tore through the bar, and out onto the street. I looked as far into the night as I could. I looked up the street, and saw them. The lights at Wrigley Field were still on. The game had ended hours ago. It didn't seem possible that the field lights would still be on, but they were. I looked at them a long time. I started crying. I hailed a cab and asked the driver to take me home. We drove past the stadium and I watched the lights as long as I could as we pulled onto Lakeshore Drive. I saw the beautiful skyline and the city lights around me. Light. I saw light.

PART THREE

Lowering a Drawbridge

From the seven-year-old, the heart...

Will you listen to me? Please? I don't want to die. We are not going to die, are we? I'm really scared right now. We are not going to do this right? Look at the coin. The man gave us the coin and we promised. We can't break a promise. It's not right to break a promise.

I'll tell you a truth. There are times when I thought I might like to die because then if I did I'd get to go to heaven and we would see Daddy and then we could be together. It's only the times when I miss him most. The times I'm hurt and broken, or when I have bad dreams. That's when I really wish he were here so that I could laugh again. Daddy always made it so I did not have to worry about all of those things. Daddy made me feel safe and protected and I know Daddy loved us no matter what.

I don't want you to be mad at me. I was really mad at you when we got sick and the doctor said we couldn't be a mother. That made me mad. You said you were doing what you thought was best and I believed you. I did. It's just that

I'm really sad and I don't know how to be less sad. But I don't think we should die. As much as I want to be with Daddy and feel safe, I don't think we should die.

I know you are the boss of me. I think it is okay to let you be the boss of me because I'm really scared and sad and don't know what to do. You are the smart one, and I listen to you most of the time. Will you listen to me now? I think we are really tired. You keep saying we don't need anyone to help us figure out how we live with everything that's happened. I think it may be time to have someone show us another way. We need to be able to talk to someone about what's happened to us and help us understand it because I don't think we are supposed to be sad or afraid all of the time. We could tell someone what we are doing and make sure we are doing it right. I think there may be some other way to do this so that we aren't scared all the time.

Daddy went away a long time ago and that changed a lot of things. There are nights where I try to guess what it would be like if he hadn't gone away. I don't know why he did. I don't know why Uncle John did, either. I don't know why we won't be able to be a mother. I don't know why we have such a hard time with things and all we seem to know how to do is work. I think there is so much more out there to do instead of work and I want to find it. I don't know why we still have really bad nightmares, way worse than when we were little.

I want to know what we are supposed to do about it. You keep telling me that I have to get over it; no one cares about how we feel. So, now I'm going to tell you a truth. I don't believe that. I think people care about us. I think we have pretended that they don't care because you don't want me to be hurt. It's not working. I want to be allowed to care about people, about things. I want to be able to be sad or mad or happy or silly and have it be all right.

I want to feel like I do when I swing really high and then I slow down because it's time to stop. Right before I stop, I'm still going, and I jump out of the swing. You have to do it just right and at just the right time so you don't fall. But I know how to do that. Well, a couple of times I fell and skinned my knees. But I know how to jump like that and when I do, there is a minute where I fly. And there's a second I don't know if I'll land or fall, but I don't care, because I'm flying. If I fall, I'll skin my knee. If I land, then I won't. But no matter what, I got to fly.

Make it feel like I feel when I can fly. And promise we will keep the promise we made to the man who gave us the coin. He made us promise and we said we would, and a promise is a promise. You can't break it. Do you promise?

CHAPTER NINE

Bridge Building

The next morning, I walked to my favorite breakfast spot and listened to everything my heart had to say. I was terrified and standing on the edge of my own life. I had taken a big step back toward life the night before, but I was an extremely dangerous place. I wasn't exactly sure what to do next. I pulled out a pad of paper and started doodling. I found four words: work, health, home, and love. I drew a circle around these and wrote the word "help" on the top, and on the bottom I wrote the words "therapy and healing." I had to find help. I used my project management experience to formulate a plan, as I had done hundreds of times before. This plan, however, was the plan to fix me. I wanted to keep taking steps away from the ledge. It was time to build a bridge and allow some people into the fortress to help me.

The first step was to find a new job. I loved Chicago, and had had the highest hopes that I could be happy there, but knew it was time to pull up stakes. I needed a short-term battle plan to deal with that office. It was toxic to me and I could not keep putting myself back on that front line. I decided I would limit my time to the exact amount of time I was needed there. It became an interesting way to force balance into work.

I needed a therapist, and promised myself to find one as soon as I secured a new job. I didn't want to start a relationship with someone and have to leave. I needed a home, but at the moment I wasn't quite sure where that would be. I didn't have a great sense of belonging anywhere in the world. Home didn't feel like a geographic area, as I felt I could live almost anywhere. Home allowed me to be fully who I was, as I was, however I was, with no judgment or fear. I had a picture in my mind of what a home was like. It was warm, inviting and safe. It had a fireplace for cold days and a big deck with comfy chairs for a warm summer evening. It was filled with love. I wondered if I would find it and told myself it would unfold after I figured out the job part.

Love - the romantic part of love - sat on the outskirts of these other issues at the moment. My track record with romance was not great, and yet I wanted this very much in my life, and I had no idea how it would come to be. My self-esteem was in the toilet. I thought so little of myself in this fragile period that it was inconceivable to think of someone else able to see me as I wanted to be seen. I was incapable of feeling worthy of that kind of love. I was afraid to reach out for love only to be hurt or rejected. My heart didn't have the strength to withstand someone leaving or hurting me. I decided to shelve this issue for the moment, and added it to the list of promises I was making regarding my work in therapy.

It was important to be in the daylight, the sun, and outside as much as possible. I was not experiencing a lot of pain or difficulty with the endometriosis at the moment, but it was a part of my life. I reminded myself of the importance of wellness as it related to exercising, following healthy diet, and minimizing stress whenever possible. My emotional well-being would be addressed through therapy. I walked to and from work every day and took the time I would have been working to exercise and run. I stayed focused on the light, the air, and my surroundings. I went to the Oak Street Beach and put my toes in the sand. I watched the boats on the Chicago River as I crossed Michigan Avenue on my walks to and from work.

I kept that coin with me everyday and kept an eye out for the man who had gifted it to me. I slept with it under my pillow. It was my constant reminder of the deal I made with that man and myself that night. I was struck by how he had seen me so clearly without knowing me at all. He cut through all of the external layers and reached in and touched my heart. I had no idea how he had done it, but I knew he had saved my life. It was a simple gift and gesture, a game token from a bar. Yet, to me, it represented the ability to find light, to keep moving, and to believe in possibility. He showed a kindness and gave me a sense of hope that I was worthy of those feelings. I decided that I was going to keep that promise and on the bad days, I kept it if only to honor him, and the moment in which he touched my heart. I promised myself that I would keep finding the light in my darkness, no matter what. I was going to keep that promise forever.

Find a Job

One day, not too long after I launched this first phase of my plan, I received an odd call from the firm I had left in Washington D.C.. I understood they had gone through a management change. They were interested in speaking with me regarding a completely different way to have me work with them. It was an internal role. I might be asked to pitch in on some consulting assignments, but my billing quota would be small and not tied to my performance. I expressed that my focus was on personal life and health. I wanted a career opportunity that would challenge me to grow as a leader and not as a machine hammering out billable hours. This could not be a gateway to an old life. We reached an agreement and within six weeks I was on my way back to Washington D.C.. I considered this carefully and in the end took the gamble to stay with the environment I knew. It was a calculated risk. I saw it as an opportunity to prove to myself that I could stand by the fire and not jump into it. I was returning to a familiar place with a network and friends and I needed that sense of security more than anything.

"What Brings You Here?"

I kept my promise and found a therapist within two weeks. For confidentiality, I'll call her Laura. Her office was right up the street from the office and I was nervous at our first appointment. I had never been to therapy, not even after my dad died. I had been raised around the idea that therapy was for *crazy people*, and I should be able to do everything myself. I thought it was complete and utter bullshit. I still think that to this day. I didn't anyone care what anyone thought. I needed help.

"What brings you here today?" Laura asked and I started crying. I told her I didn't want to die. I was twenty-nine years old, and I didn't know how to live. Those were the first moments of an almost ten-year relationship with her. The first sessions were rough. My mind was fighting as the emotions choked and stammered out of me. I was afraid at first to let her see me cry. I didn't know how to be real with my emotions. As a child, it had been ingrained to mask and hide what I was feeling and always be "fine." Crying was something I got into trouble for doing. This became my first lesson in therapy. Emotions are a part of the human construct, go ahead and cry. I soon came to trust that in that room, in that chair, I was allowed to talk about anything and anyone.

I needed to understand what had happened to me in a way that my mind could process. Laura taught me about conditions like post-traumatic stress disorder, depression, co-dependency, and narcissism. Defense mechanisms like avoidance, denial, and projection were described. I learned how addictive and compulsive behaviors form in response to abuse. I had been the victim of verbal and emotional abuse. We touched on my repressed memories enough to know that it was too soon to go there. She explained that a repressed memory was gone from the conscious mind yet remained active in the subconscious mind. It was highly plausible I reacted to conditions or situations as if I remembered them, except I didn't. When I could not connect a reaction or response to something, the root cause was contained within the repressed memory.

All of those conditions and mechanisms were swirling around my life; they were a part of who I was.

I was suffering from a long and latent form of post-traumatic stress disorder. I was co-dependent; at the mercy of managing and supporting other's emotions, at the expense of my own. As an independent adult, it was easy for me to deny my own emotions in a situation to focus on anyone else's. The only person that mattered in that room with Laura was me. It was a first and it took some getting used to.

Clinically speaking, Laura clarified, I was depressed. My life had spun out into a dark and scary place. I was off the ledge but still on a steep, narrow path back to safer territory. It felt like I was crossing between two cliffs. I was working my way back to the safer cliff, but the bridge was old and unstable. It could break at any minute and I would go plummeting into the rocky ravine. I was lost, alone, and afraid. I was sad and angry. I missed my father and uncle. I was questioning every choice I had ever made in my life, and desperately wanted to understand what I do now. I craved the support and love of people, yet lacked the capacity to understand how to create and sustain intimate relationships. Therapy was *requiring* my emotions to come forward and encouraging me to *experience* feelings that I had kept locked away. I didn't trust that I was equipped to connect with my emotions. I had been conditioned to block and avoid feeling, and I was afraid of what would happen when I actually began the *work* of feeling.

I was a mess. I heard myself describe the traumatic events I remembered (to this point), and in this, found the first glimmers of understanding the intense magnitude of what I had experienced. I knew early on that therapy was a significant commitment. I would be in session once or twice a week and sometimes for several hours at a time. It was time to look at me, the whole me, and start to figure out how I was going to live now. There were sessions where I did nothing but cry; others where my defense mechanisms pushed me into a corner. I spent the time in between reflecting on what I was learning about myself. I immersed myself in the study of these conditions and behaviors and this fueled my motivation to continue. I was connecting dots in my life, choices, and behaviors. When I was sad or concentrating on something difficult, I reminded myself that everything I was learning and everything I was feeling was for me.

We decided to start at the top. My first therapy "project" was to learn how to grieve. I had never grieved for my father or uncle. I was stuck in shock, denial, and sadness with my dad, and anger toward my uncle. I needed to create a process that allowed me to put these milestone traumas in context. The seven-year-old girl showed up during many of these sessions as my heart seeped pain, sadness, loneliness, and despair. My heart was afraid to be mad because of the fear of getting into "trouble" as I had been threatened as a child. Laura created a safe space for me to explore my anger, to get mad, and to learn how to process the emotions that come with anger. She gently nudged me back into my own space of emotion any time I would drift to someone else's. I had supported other people's emotions at the expense of my own, and it was time to change this behavior.

The challenge in therapy was my mind. I was smart, and I had used my intelligence as a part of my protective shield. I had to teach myself to "stand down" and allow my emotions to come through. It was Laura's job to help me find ways to get my head out of the way and open a space to heal. Laura created an educational context to my emotional landscape. She was pragmatic and at times blunt in her approach. This was not a "how does that make you feel" type of therapeutic relationship. She learned quickly that my ego was fiercely protecting my heart, and how my mind was controlling all aspects of my emotions and guarding them tightly.

She was brilliant. Instead of challenging my mind or attempting to dismiss its relevance and value to me in this highly emotional process, she worked with it. She battled with my head on an intellectual level to create a framework, an understanding for what was happening, and what had happened. She kept it as cut and dry as possible. She didn't challenge the ego I had created. She respected it, and she worked with it. She approached the deepest parts of my pain, not through my heart, but through my *head*. When my head was satisfied it understood something, she was able to help my tender heart seep emotion. She asked me to drop the drawbridge. Let her in to let her help me grieve, release, and relieve. Let the mind work, then let the heart heal. It was a beautiful dance, and we danced like this for years.

There were moments where I broke down completely. I fell flat on my face. I got in my own way all the time. Frustration became common when I hit a brick wall. I needed to sleep for days to recover from the intensity. There were times I left the office happy for making a connection and others darkened by the slow and sometimes extremely tedious process and progress. In time, there was a little less fight and a little more calm. I was still high-spirited, opinionated and stubborn. My ego was still way out in front leading the charge, but there was a softer side slowly sneaking its way into my consciousness. My heart was finding more opportunities and openings to be heard.

After a few months working together, Laura asked me what I believed in most. I declared without skipping a beat, "love." It was one of the rare moments I actually saw her tear up. She said, "You believe in love?"

"I have to, because if I don't believe in it, then there's nothing for me to believe. Nothing to hold onto on the days that still seem so dark and sad. I'm over. So I have to believe in it. Despite everything that's happened to me. I have to believe that love exists and that I'm capable of giving and having it in my life."

A Difficult Choice

My health issues settled into a pattern. There were moments when I had debilitating pain from the endometriosis to such an extreme extent that I wasn't able to walk by the day's end. I agreed to a more aggressive, highly effective drug treatment plan that would minimize this pain for up to a year at a time. During the moments I was not experiencing pain, I was as physically active as I could be. I ran and exercised, and felt the greatest sense of balance in these moments. I started working with a personal trainer, and this helped me keep my body as strong as possible as I navigated the pain-induced ups and downs. When I was pain free, we pushed the edge of my physical capacity, if for no other reason than to prepare my body for the inevitable return of pain and treatment.

I was in full awareness that each round of drug treatment took me further away from that remote chance to have my own children. The statistics had not been with me and they continued to dwindle down to nothing. I decided that the best strategy for me was to follow any course that would leave me as physically pain free as possible. As I crossed into my thirties, my therapist sat across from me, and we started to unravel the profound emptiness, sadness, anger, guilt, and shame I felt for the loss of this choice.

A Holding Pattern on Addiction

I started to see work a little differently in these next years. I tried to figure out what I needed to complete my professional picture. I looked at my career as a pie; the slices represented things like education, subject matter expertise, leadership/management, etc. I deliberately sought opportunities that would allow me to fill out the slices. I shifted focus to what I needed to do to complete *me*, not to complete a company. I began to see me as a person with a personal *and* professional persona. I realized I had a capacity to have more than work in my life. I didn't know how to do it, but I was learning.

I was still a powerhouse worker, and living in a "white knuckle" sobriety phase of my addiction. I wasn't convinced that I had a problem with work. I had a problem with putting myself in situations where work performance was a dominating requirement. I needed to fix this and then I would be fine. I convinced myself that my new approach would work. I forced balance into my life. I put appointments on my calendar for personal things like exercise. I created rules to reflect what I thought I needed for a personal life and tried to follow them. It was as if my personal life was a "to do "list and I kept adding to the list. I believed as long as I had things to check off, I had "personal" tasks, I was a living a balanced life, and I didn't have a problem with work.

My hopes for a markedly different future at the consulting firm dwindled in the first few months. The firm called me back to the line of duty to bill more hours. I felt as if I was military reserve and they were reactivating me. It was time to leave. I had to keep the space in my life to get better. Therapy was working and I became the priority in my life, not work. I knew it was time to cut and run again, and find a new work assignment.

I found another opportunity in Washington D.C.. The company sold technology solutions and I managed a group that supported custom projects. I would fortify the management and leadership "slices" of my career pie. I found it to be an almost perfect job for me. It brought my expertise together in a way that made me feel complete. It was demanding, but this company had a lifestyle focus. People worked and had lives. I had to travel, but could set parameters around this, and it wouldn't interfere as much with my personal time. My colleagues were all in similar age/life spaces and we had a lot of fun both in and out of work. Of all my business experiences, this was one of my happiest.

I was working on an assignment with a large client. It came to the attention of management that the client was looking for something that aligned with a new product line the company was developing. The executive team wondered if the client would be willing to be a prototype for this new product. The client agreed to explore the approach as long as they had the option to revert back to the original plan. Internally, a political battle ensued regarding project control and it seemed like the client and I got caught in the middle. I took a protective stance over the client's objectives for success with this initiative. In the end, it seemed I found myself ensnared in a nasty battle and I lost. One day, my boss and the HR director walked into my office and I was fired.

As I sat there, the protective ten-year-old came forward. I was calm and collected as I listened to their words. I buried all emotions and kept a professional stance. I protected myself as they reviewed a separation agreement. I told them I was distraught and confused and I wouldn't sign anything under duress. I told them I would be back to pack up my office and no one should touch a thing. They agreed to honor my requests. I needed to speak with my attorney.

I made it as far as the parking garage and I broke down. I was shocked and in utter disbelief. Everything had been going great. I loved the job. I was struck down at what seemed the precise moment I was relaxing into my life. I cursed myself a little as I realized I had let my guard down. I allowed myself to believe I could be happy. Life relented and refused, and took what I wanted away. I arrived home and sat on my couch for a long time and considered what might happen next. I began to shut down and retreat within myself to deal with the emotional waves that were swelling as shock gave way to reality. I was alone in that moment, but I wouldn't be for long.

I received a call that people were on their way to my house. Eight of my friends and work colleagues showed up with supplies. They ordered a bunch of food from an Italian restaurant and while two of them put a spread out for everyone, another pair wrapped all of the extra food they bought for leftovers. Someone had gone to the grocery store and brought things they knew I liked. They stocked my pantry and freezer. There was at least a case of wine to share and more to spare for later. I watched as I allowed these people in my home, life, and my trauma. They helped me. My phone rang non-stop as people heard the news and reached out to let me know they cared and were there for me. We ate and drank and laughed. I found the power of laughter through tears for the first time in my life. I left the bridge down and *allowed* them to cross. I went to bed uncertain and afraid. I looked for the voices that once would have told me no one cared and my feelings didn't matter. I couldn't hear them. I only heard laughter.

I was devastated by what happened to me. I used the grieving process I had learned in therapy to manage the trauma. Work had always been my stability and this experience showed me that it was not something to trust anymore. I found another job quickly, but my attitude changed. It forced a perspective in my life, and I had the strength and support of therapy to help me navigate this very slippery slope. I lost ground in some aspects of my emotional healing and gained ground in others. One day, I received a call from an old friend. The Managing Partner of that consulting firm, the same firm that had hired me and brought me to D.C. from Cleveland. That firm had now disbanded, and a group of six had started their own firm. This was "lifestyle consulting," not the high-strung, frenzied culture of the prior firm. This was the opportunity to be a consultant *and* have a life. Would I like to join them?

   The protector...

   I think we should take this job. I know you think it's risky going back, but I think we should. We know these people and I don't trust where we are now. I think it's time we go back and try this one more time. We will still go to therapy and be able to work on all of the emotional stuff. I think it's helping. We know how to work better now. We have friends, we do things; and it's getting better. I love being a consultant. I know how to do it, and out of all the jobs we have had it's the one that always comes back to us and I think we should listen. I think this is exactly what we need right now. We can settle in and build a life around this. Have a life and be a consultant. Won't that make both of us happy?

CHAPTER TEN

Open the Doors

I took the job and settled into a routine. I liked the idea that it was a small company. It was like having my own business, except I wasn't alone. We were all contributing and there was a management hierarchy, but it had an independent feel to it. There was a partner structure and I had been offered a six-month vesting process. I had considered starting my own business after I was fired, but was too nervous about how I would survive and provide for myself. This seemed a good compromise and I was hopeful that this would be a great beginning.

I took the plunge and bought my first house in 1999. This was the first place where I felt a sense of a real home. It was mine. I bought, decorated, and loved it. It was in a quaint and quirky historic neighborhood called Old Town. I loved walking to the farmers' market on the weekends; I felt a great sense of belonging somewhere. My neighbors were great and we did lots of things together. My health had improved greatly, and the disease was well-managed and quiet for the time being. There was a running trail less than a mile away from my home. I ran long stretches along the Potomac River and took in all the sites of Washington D.C. It was a happy time. I was going with it.

Remembering

The summer of 2000, on a random Friday night, I was on the phone with my brother when he shared his perspective regarding how he thought my father died. He didn't believe his death had been an accident, rather a suicide. I don't remember how our conversation got to there, but it did. For some reason, he thought I already knew and believed the same. Off the phone, I trembled and broke down. I was back in the funeral home standing at my father's coffin. Hearing those words sent a shockwave through my body and a jolting current through my mind as I struggled to process what I had heard.

My seven-year-old heart cried...

Daddy... I'm so sorry Daddy. I didn't know you were so sad. You didn't seem sad to me. I'm so sorry Mom hurt you like that. Were you afraid you weren't going to see us anymore? It's so hard to imagine what that must have been like for you. I was so sad and it was dark for me in my life when I was in Chicago, but then that man stepped in and saved me. I can't imagine how dark it must have been for you. I wish there had been someone there to save you. I wish I had been able to save you. I'm so sorry. I wish you were here. I wish you knew how much I was going to miss you before you left and I wish that would have been enough to make you want to stay. It got so crazy after you left. You always took care of me and then you were gone. Did you know I looked for you everywhere I went? I wanted you to come home. I was so scared. Did you know I was going to be so scared? Please tell me you didn't want me to be scared and alone. I miss you so much and I love you.

I called my therapist and left a message with her service, and I poured a drink. Then I poured another, and then another. There was not enough alcohol in my house to numb the pain. My crying plateaued, and in that quiet moment, it happened. I started to remember. The floodgates opened. A dark, dark night gave way to a blinding light. It felt a little like getting up in the middle of the night and flipping the bathroom light switch and you are momentarily blinded. It was like that, times a thousand.

I couldn't control what was happening. I was seeing many things, hearing many voices, and feeling a tremendous amount of pain. It was unbearable. My head throbbed as if my brain was literally expelling memories and they were ramming into my skull. The phone rang; it was Laura. I could barely speak, but I managed to share the conversation with my brother and how that had triggered memory recall. Help. She asked if I needed to go to the hospital? No. Come see her in the morning. First thing. Okay. I hung up the phone and passed out.

We spent three hours together that morning. My heart just poured; I had no ability to control what was happening. Did I want something for the anxiety? No, on this I was clear. I was going to feel every moment of this. I wasn't going to numb this, mask this, or block it out. Those memories had been hiding in the deep recesses of my mind and I was being set free. I wasn't going to do anything to stop it. I was going to get to the raw edge of my emotions. I was going to put this all together. I promised to call if I thought I was losing it, but I wasn't going to lose it. I had just started to find it and I wasn't going to let go.

I had to grieve for my father, again. I had had my own experiences with suicide, and was fearful that I might find myself back on that edge. I wondered how was I going to stay off that ledge? I did not want to relapse. If his death *was* a suicide, I wanted to confront my mother and have her tell us what she thought. I recalled him telling me he wouldn't do it. We wouldn't be believed and if I was going to do it despite his objection, I would be on my own. He asked me to keep this secret between us.

I also was in the first stages of memory recovery. The initial memories were centered on the rage, anger, and verbal and emotional abuse. The memories came back in waves. Sometimes I would get a complete perspective, and at other times it was only glimmers, shadows, or images. I might get a sound, a smell, or a feeling as a single sensation or in combination. I had to tell my mind and the protective mechanisms to yield. The protector within me needed to permit the memory to restore and allow the heart to feel the experience. It was confusing at first and in time, a process emerged from the chaos. My process of recovering memories involved three distinct elements.

The first was to discern the difference between an attributed memory and a recovered one, because I had both. An attributed memory was one where I attached myself to someone else's "story" of what happened. For example, if someone talked about a vacation and I didn't remember it, I would learn to remember it as they told it and then I would tell it the same. A recovered memory, or a memory in recovery process, was different for one key reason. I could *feel or sense* something. I had an emotion around the event whatever it was. If I could feel it, it was real. That was step one.

After that, the focus of my effort was creating awareness. I kept a journal with me and took it everywhere I went. I kept track of the things I remembered and what triggered me to recall the memory. Sometimes it was a flash or an image, sometimes it was the way someone said something or the way I responded to how someone said something. At first, the deliberate focus on and awareness of so many things was exhausting. I felt as if I had to be plugged into everything I said and did. I wrote pages at the end of the day to catalog what I did and what I remembered. I filled notebooks in days. I kept a notepad by my bed and searched for things in my dreams when my brain would be quiet.

The last thing I needed was patience. Recovering memories is a painstaking process. A memory recovery could take days, weeks, months, or years.

Forcing a recovery could cause severe damage. It could interfere with the recovery of other memories. My mind had been keeping things from me for a *reason*. My subconscious mind would let my conscious self know only when it was ready to deal with it. This was one inner conflict between the ten-year-old protector and me as the adult. I wouldn't know this until almost fourteen years later. What I did know was that I needed to respect the process and be patient. I was not a patient person, and I spent those first moments frustrated with myself. The more frustrated I became, the more I locked myself out of the one thing I wanted - to remember. I learned to be patient if only with this part of my life.

As I brought a memory into light, I examined it with Laura in a therapeutic setting. Some of those memories were events, vacations, parties, and other non-threatening moments. The worst memories were the moments of rage, anger, and the verbal and emotional abuse. I could hear screaming and felt be grabbed by my arms and shook. I heard the door slams, and the rush of fear when I recalled the door re-opening for one last burst of anger. I smelled the alcohol and tasted bile with those good night kisses. I could touch my tears as I cried quietly in my room. Those were the first days of what would become an almost fifteen year journey in recovering the lost eight years that I had blacked out from my childhood.

A Daring Choice

I needed time and space to sort through everything that was happening to me. I needed to protect myself from the likelihood that I would backspin into that dark space. I also had a big choice to make with respect to work. I had partnership papers in my hand to review and sign. I was hesitant. I was nervous regarding the firm's future and what would happen if I was a partner and it experienced financial challenges. I had obligations. I also needed time and space to rebuild myself and dig out from this emotional landslide. The demand and the pressure to generate revenue had increased overtime and fueled my concerns. The message was clear that time off work was not an option. Billing and generating revenue was. We all had to step up to the plate. I teetered on the edge as I contemplated. I could jump back into the working frenzy and use it to hide, or I could walk away from the edge and focus on what my heart needed instead.

I made my choice. I walked into the Managing Partner's office and presented her with the partnership papers, unsigned. My office was already packed. I thanked them for the opportunity and wished them great success in their future. It was time to focus on me, *all of me.*

A Fresh Start

I put together my own little consulting business. Total employees… one. Me. I found a couple of projects which kept the bills paid and provided me with the freedom to explore all of those things that were hitting me at once. I expected to find a full-time job and remained actively in search. I realized six months later that I already had my new job. I kept my eye out for opportunities, but I liked the feeling of being my own boss. The work was steady and the business grew. I subcontracted a project to build a small software application to an old friend I worked with years before. We had always worked well together and this was no exception. When we finished that project, we agreed to keep going, and work together in partnership. I kept finding projects that allowed us to build the business.

I continued my work in therapy. The first wave of recovered memories slowed in time. The process became less intense as I became more comfortable with what was happening to me. I continued to have moments and episodes, but none as severe in those first weeks my initial recovery process was triggered.

It was at this time that love found me. I have kept the details of romantic love from this story as I think it's a story all its' own and best told another day. I introduce romantic love here, as it was then, that I met the man I thought I would marry; and it seemed that my life was coming together. I was happy, and was like this for a few years.

And then, a slow downward spiral began. That man left me for another woman. He was not faithful to me during our relationship. His leaving broke my heart into a million pieces. It was the trigger for my broken heart to flee back into the darkness of the castle to hide. The protector led me back to the safety and avoidance that came with work. After almost seven years, I was falling off the wagon. A dormant addiction was waking as I spun back to a place where I felt safe. Work.

CHAPTER ELEVEN

A New Castle, An Old Habit

From the protector...

Well... I hope you are happy. See? Do you see now what happens when you get ahead of yourself and think you know better? You fall in love. You think he's going to marry you. He cheats. He leaves. He picks her over you.

Let's face it, do you really think you are cut out for love? Do you really think you know what you are doing? Do you really think anyone will want to be with you long term? We are a mess. We are damaged. Every time we think we are happy, something happens, and someone leaves. We have to live with all of this crap. No one else does. I think if we learned anything from this last experience it is that love is really something that is just out of reach. No one wants to be with our mess. Best to cut our losses and take a different course.

It's time for a fresh start. A new place to live. There are too many reminders and memories here. It looks like this little business of ours is making progress, so let's find somewhere a little more affordable where we don't have to worry so much about things.

I think it's best to let this business be our focus. I can work hard and it won't be like before. The harder I work, the more money I make and the more we can have what we want in our life. Well, everything except love. You really need to give that up. Focus on the business, it's what I do, it's what I'm good at. Stop worrying about all that other crap.

I'll find you a new castle. We can have a house, a real house, with a yard. Big enough that we could spend all of our time in it if we wanted and not feel cramped. We will start fresh. No one will know us.

I kept my promise after Chicago. I agreed to get someone to help us and the therapist has been a good investment. I promise you I'll fix this and you will be fine. In fact, you will be better than fine because of all the new great stuff I know. Now it's your turn. Promise me you will give up on this stupid love stuff for once and for all. It's not who we are. Do you promise?

My Castle

After a little research, I settled on Durham, North Carolina as home. The business didn't tie me to a specific location as long as I had access to an airport. Durham seemed a perfect blend of the places I had lived. It was a small, friendly town. In this, it felt a little like my hometown of Cleveland. Duke University and the University of North Carolina kept a high concentration of educated, professional people in residence. It was relatively sophisticated from a cultural and lifestyle perspective. In this, it felt a little like Washington D.C. and Chicago. I thought it a good compromise.

I built a house in a growing part of town. I made it everything I ever wanted to have in a home. It had a front porch with two big rocking chairs. It had vaulted ceilings, an open floor plan, and lots of windows. Natural light was important to me and I added windows everywhere I could. It had a fireplace in the great room to take the chill off a cool Carolina winter morning or evening. The kitchen was the focal point and it opened onto a large great room; it was my creative space. I was blessed with the cooking and baking genes from my father's mother. I found a sense of peace when I was in the kitchen bringing something to life and sharing it with someone. I decorated the house in warm brown and taupe tones, contrasted with bright white plantation shutters and trim. I used deep reds, greens, and earth tones to bring color and calm. There were big puffy couches and chairs, the kind to sink into with a big mug of tea or glass of wine.

I loved to entertain and this home was made for it. My two favorite parties were during the holidays. I put less focus on the painful days – Christmas Eve and New Year's Eve – and created my own traditions. The night before Thanksgiving, I hosted the Red Balls party. I cooked dinner and my friends and I decorated my Christmas tree. My tree was different than the trees I had as young child. There were no ornaments marking a life's milestone, or a child's creative use of popsicle sticks. My Christmas tree was decorated with red and silver balls and accents of glass and crystal snowflakes and icicles. A big bow on the top was the last step. What made my tree distinct and beautiful was the *experience* shared with my friends. I kept the tree exactly as it was decorated that night, whether it met my aesthetic standards or not. That tree served a constant reminder of the power of friendship, laughter, and love. It carried me through the season and became a healing tradition.

I addressed the difficulties of New Year's Eve, and decided to end and begin a year doing things I loved with people I loved. I spent the evening of

New Year's Eve in the kitchen, preparing a traditional southern feast that I would share with friends on New Year's Day. It was complete with collard greens, black-eyed peas, cream corn, ham, corn bread, and a big side of football. There was always something spicy and something super sweet to wish us balance in the year ahead. Slippers and sweatpants were the dress code, and if anyone had a resolution to get healthy, they might want to start January 2nd. Inevitably, we ended up around my kitchen table contemplating the year ahead. We shared our hopes, goals, and even our fears and worries as we set off into the New Year. I loved how these conversations started from the exact place we left it the year before. No matter how many times we had gathered in between, we picked right up from the year before. It became one of my favorite days of the year.

After each party, when the house was cleaned up, I took a moment and enjoyed the warm, rich, energy that lingered. I poured my last glass of wine and sunk into my huge tub for a nice long soak. I wound down from the festivities amidst the glow of candlelight. I made my own wishes as I inhaled the scents of vanilla and sandalwood bubble bath. I crawled into my big mahogany sleigh bed, wrapped myself in soft sheets and cozy blankets, and drifted off to sleep.

My house in Durham was the closest of all the places I had lived that felt like a real home. It was the actual castle I created for my heart to hide from the world. It was simple and quiet and it was mine. It was my sanctuary and cocoon. It provided me the safety and comfort I needed from a world that had given me a pretty good beating.

The Family I Chose

Before I left Washington D.C., I decided I needed something in my life to help my broken heart. I needed to love something that I knew only knew how to love me back. I named her Sophie because I always loved that name for a little girl. A seven-pound, tiny toy poodle and sharp contrast to the big retrievers I had growing up. Sophie fit my lifestyle and she was a master overachiever in the art of unconditional love. A few years later, Sophie and I rescued an orange and white tabby cat, and I named him Finnegan. He taught me what it meant to be adored. He crossed a room to meet me, threw his paws around my neck, and hugged me tight. Sophie and Finnegan gave my heart something to love and care for the best I knew. Together we became a little family.

I found great friends in Durham and they became another addition to the family I chose. Most were transplants like me. It was a great, eclectic mix of people, places, and activities. We shared many great times together.

I was at arm's length from my actual family. I might get to Cleveland once a year to visit. Most of my experiences were via email and phone calls. I was at odds with my mother and brother. I struggled with this whole "secret" regarding my father. It became more difficult to spend time as I perpetuated this denial; I felt disrespectful to my dad. The family dynamic slowly eroded. My relationship with my brother broke first. He came to live with me for a while. I came to find a rage similar to the memories I had recovered from our time together as children. He left one night after a brutal argument. I had locked myself in my own room out of fear he would hurt me. It would be seven years before I would see him again.

My tenuous relationship with my mother further deteriorated during the next couple of years. I sensed in her a strong alignment with my brother. It seemed to me she was believing and choosing him over me. I believed that if the three of us were standing on a cliff and someone told my mother that she had to choose which one of us had to go, my mother would push me off the cliff and save herself and my brother. From my perspective, that was our family dynamic. I felt an odd sense of relief with this distance and breakdown in these relationships.

Status Quo

I continued with therapy and worked with Laura remotely. Our sessions had tapered to every other week and then once a month. After almost ten years, I had absorbed almost all the benefit I could from therapy. My memory recovery slowed and the recovery process itself became fluid and ingrained in my life. It became a second nature of sorts and I grew comfortable with the unpredictable patterns that emerged when a memory restored. This slowing was my mind's way of telling me that there had been enough for the time being.

I struggled with the night terrors that had set in as a child. The ones where someone was dragging me were the worst. I felt like I was digging my heels into quicksand, I couldn't get traction and I sank and became trapped. I was immobile and helpless, and I screamed to let me wake up. I screamed for my dad. When I woke up, my heart raced, I felt the energy around me and looked deep into the night to see what I could see. It was always black. It took a long time for the horror to subside. I lay awake for hours after these episodes and wonder when they would pass. These weren't the nightmares of a child grown into adulthood. These were the nightmares of a troubled, broken soul.

I knew these terrors had something to do with the black that blocked my memories. I took these episodes into therapy to no avail. There was no movement and in time, I came to settle into the reality that this was a part of who I was. My memory would let me know when it was ready to remember; until then, time and patience were my strategies.

My health continued on an up and down cycle and I was on and off drug treatments as needed to manage the endometriosis. I was in my late thirties and conversations evolved from drug options to more permanent surgical ones. The doctors felt it was important for me to get as far into my forties as possible before surgery, and I settled into a wait game.

My body was fragile, my heart was broken, and I was convinced I was not equipped or worthy of having love in my life. My heart yielded to the protector. The shields and barriers remained in place and that little girl stayed tucked away in the castle where she felt safe. She was alone and lonely, but she was safe, and that's what was important at the moment. I didn't have it in me to take another risk on love. My life would be work-centered and I settled into a life building what I thought I wanted through my business.

Reaching a Milestone

In 2007, I turned forty and celebrated in Sonoma, CA with a group of close friends. I was on an up-cycle and more than a little happy to send my thirties packing. I welcomed this new decade in grand style. I found something I hadn't known I was looking for amongst the vineyards, bold cabernets, and soft pinot noirs. I met my spiritual self courtesy of a sweet, kind, and intuitive woman named Jenna Rae.

I spent my birthday at the resort spa and capped off a beautiful day with a spa treatment that included an astrology reading and then a chakra healing meditation. The Hindus believe Chakras are centers of energies within our body. These energy zones align from the base of our spine (root) to the top of our head (crown) and it's widely believed there are seven. Chakra healing practices seek to clear and balance each zone and in doing so create a stronger sense of harmony and balance across mental, physical, and spiritual aspects of the self.[2]

Jenna Rae went through my astrological chart. She started her reading telling me I was highly creative, and had an abundance of energy. There was a lot of power and passion in my chart. I had been presented many challenges in my life and they were here for a purpose. I was extremely intuitive and needed to live more into the spiritual calling of my life. I would understand more at some future point. Now was the time to begin exploring and learning. I chose seven crystals. She then associated these crystals with each energy zone and guided me through a healing meditation. I felt a tingling sensation and clarity as we worked from the base of my spine to the top of my head. I emerged from this session feeling refreshed and rejuvenated, as if I had woken from a sleep that had lasted for years.

I picked up all the books she suggested and began my study of spirituality. Jenna Rae gave me permission to see into the unseen, explore the realms of spiritual belief, and create my own practice. She sparked a curiosity and showed me the way onto the path. I slowly took those first tentative steps. I reached into this milestone with the hope this next decade of my life would be my best ever and that things might finally come together. But first, I had to get back to work.

The Rational Addict

Working from home allowed me to quietly revive the workaholic behaviors that protected me from the life I was afraid to live. I was alone most days and my interactions were mostly phone conversations and conference calls. I remotely connected to the world and in these first years with my heart broken as it was, I felt safe. I convinced myself that my life was in balance because I had time to keep up with the routine tasks like gym, laundry, chores, and cooking. I had forced time into my life for these personal "things" and considered this a huge step forward in my life. I was able to have the life I wanted, as long as I brought my laptop and cellphone / PDA with me everywhere just in case someone needed something. I described it as the trade-off that was necessary to have the life I wanted, and this was a lie. These were my security blankets.

This relapse phase of my addiction was subtle. It wasn't about billing hundreds of hours, staying up all night, working seven days a week and travelling five of them. This was living in a constant, ready-state to be there when the business needed me. It was right upstairs. I was always ready to jump in when needed. I was taking any emotional fulfillment from my work. I was exhausted from all of the heartbreak in my life. I had used work to fill that space in me that wasn't able to trust in love anymore. Work was the part of my life that I always understood. I wasn't driven to succeed. My drive was a fear of failing at the one thing I could always do, work.

I had a built-in set of excuses to avoid anything as a result of work demands. I was a small business owner. When there was business to be had and revenue to earn, I had best step-up and earn it because I didn't know if and when it would be there again. The addict in me did what it could to make the most of every opportunity. I saw the direct rewards of my efforts. I became completely consumed by the business; and once again it became the center of my identity and self esteem. Most every aspect of my life was connected to the business and most every conversation I had involved my business or my area of career expertise. There was no separation between work and personal space. I had an excuse for every habit, and an excuse for each toxic choice I made to hide in my work.

Work was the one part of my life I fully understood. My company grew, and I took satisfaction in my accomplishments. I had great relationships with my clients, and many had become friends. My business partner was located more than six hours away. We maintained our own space and worked virtually. I considered him among my dearest friends and confidants. We experienced many of life's joys and sorrows together and seemed to continue to step forward. Our skill sets were quite complimentary skill sets and there was little conflict in our relationship. When we decided to work together, we agreed our business would have three core ideals. First, that we provided an exceptional service to our clients. The client always came first. Second, our revenue goals were to generate enough income to support reasonable lifestyles and greed would not rule our business. The goal was to create a lifestyle we could sustain without the excessive pressure to work hundreds of hours in a week. Third, there was no 'holy grail' – we weren't in search of some huge payout. If it showed up, great, but it wasn't our mission to seek it.

We stumbled onto an opportunity to create a piece of software that would become a product we could sell. Our business had a solid revenue stream from professional services, and slowly we evolved it to include licensed-based, annuity revenue. From that point, our software evolved to a web-based solution. Suddenly, we had a technology. We had an asset. Rule number three said we would not search for the Holy Grail, but it may have found us. How would we respond? Our business was changing. The question was...were we seeing the evolution in the same way?

Rock Bottom (Again)

As the business became more complicated, my work became more intense. I was co-owner of a technology company with a new commodity. The business was highly competitive, client relationships were tricky to establish, and long-term relationships were the prize. The stress and pressure to perform and deliver was immense. I stepped up to the plate.

As I had in my twenties, I was firing on all cylinders. We were in an aggressive sales mode to sell our new service and stabilize our cash flow. The manic undertones of my work behavior returned as the uptick in pace required me to focus a more significant effort into the company's growth. The rush of adrenaline returned as I uncovered or advanced an opportunity. We were the little guys and when we stood the chance to beat one of the big ones, it fed the high that I needed from work. I tried to stay on the high as much as possible; yet, I was feeling like there were new expectations, new assumptions, and new criteria. I didn't feel the sense of appreciation I always had with my partner. It seemed an iron curtain was forging between us.

The crash snuck up on me this time. It was masked by all the rationalizations of owning the business and how the flexibility working from home implied a balance in my life. I started to see my life as this murky swampland. One day just rolled into the next and I never felt I had freedom from work. It was an interesting inner conflict. A voice deep inside me was challenging the way I had rationalized my life. I wanted it this way, but after a few years it started to wear on me. I started to wonder if this pattern was all I'd ever know for the rest of my life. If so, how much longer could I go on?

I grew increasingly tired. I felt like everyone else was on a forward path and I was stuck. My father and uncle died at thirty-five and forty, respectively. I was now in the same age range and began to feel like I was living on borrowed time. There seemed a growing void and one that I couldn't dismiss any longer. I wasn't making the connection that I desperately needed to feel complete. I had real questions concerning my purpose and even bigger ones with respect to how truly happy I was and if I even knew what happiness meant. It seemed like I had landed back in a miserable, dangerous spot where I had been before. Not satisfied, feeling like work was the only thing in front of me, and missing personal aspirations.

I was growing impatient and frustrated. Owning and licensing technology was a far more complex business and required additional contingencies and efforts to maintain and support. I was sensing an increasing resistance from my business partner regarding his obligations and commitments to the company. We were in growth mode and we needed to keep hitting our marks. I needed a break, I knew I needed a break; I just didn't know when it would come. One evening, I commiserated over dinner and drinks with some small business-owning friends. It was a rule to turn off cell phones if at all possible. I walked out to the parking lot feeling better after a great dose of laughter and assurances that I was not alone. I turned on my phone, and there it was, my breaking point.

A prospective client had been trying to reach me. The prospect had left me numerous text and voice messages saying only that I needed to call ASAP, urgent matter. It was new business for the firm. I wasn't there when he called. I felt the tightness in my throat. It was well past business hours and I called. At least he would know that I had called as soon as it had come to my attention. He picked up and we chatted. There was no emergency; the matter could have waited until normal hours.

I was angry, not with him, with me. I was dealing with his sense of urgency, his need for attention, and his definition of important. I couldn't walk away. I had to respond. This wasn't a one-time occurrence. This was the way I lived. I lived to be available for that call, at whatever moment it came, I could be there and take care of it. I waited to be needed. I had responded to his call because it made *me* feel needed. I had nothing else that mattered more to me in my life at that moment beyond the business. I hated it and hated me for living this way. I didn't know how to change. The dark, the bleak, the gray, the inability to feel was back. I was on empty and didn't know what to do next.

The next morning I looked in the mirror. My face and eyes were swollen from hours of crying and the wine I had consumed. I was tired in a way that was all too familiar. The exhaustion deep in my bones, nerves, and cells that moving was a challenge. I crawled upstairs to my office and called my business partner. I needed a break. I was completely fried. I desperately needed a moment to regroup and sort through some things. I wasn't going to wallow in this world anymore. I was disgusted with myself for who I was and I wanted to change. I didn't have the first clue how, but I was motivated to try and figure it out. The first step was a legitimate break, even if only for a few days.

I needed a place that was close enough that I could escape, but far enough I would feel like I was away. It took a few hours and then I remembered a friend telling me about Sedona. The deal was four days, no laptop, and no checking email. I was going "off the grid" for the first time in nearly nine years. I was giving myself four days to unfry my brain, find myself, and put my life back on the right path to happiness. No problem, right? Piece of cake.

CHAPTER TWELVE

Opening a New Door

The Best Laid Plans

I agreed to check messages when I landed in Phoenix. I turned on my phone and there it was. That pending sales opportunity was back. He had called my partner while I was flying from Durham to Phoenix. The prospect needed some information for a meeting at the end of the following week. He had not returned my calls for weeks, and now his projected "crisis" came at the precise moment I was trying to shake free. I was proud of my first reaction, I called my partner and told him this would be my first priority when I returned. The information I needed to review was on my laptop and I didn't have it with me. The prospect would have everything he needed in time for the meeting. I would send a quick email or leave a message explaining this to the prospect before I hit the road.

It didn't seem to me that my choice was received well by my partner. What transpired was our first major argument since we started working together. I was surprised that he didn't appear to me to be more supportive of my need for time away. I heard him dismiss my choice to follow-up when I returned. I heard him question my commitment to the company; this was new business and I should care more. The call ended with my screaming that I would take care of it somehow, someway. I threw my Blackberry across the car. I was enraged with him, with me, with life.

I began searching for a cliff with the intent to chuck my Blackberry® as far as I could. I also was pretty sure that I would go off right after it. I didn't find one. I pulled into the resort, handed the keys to the valet and took a few deep breaths hoping it would settle me. He asked me if I was okay. I told him no, really, no. I was shaken to my core. He took care of the car and bags and helped me into the lobby.

He took my bags to the suite, and put them in my bedroom. He turned on the fireplace and left for a moment, returning with ice. He opened a bottle of water and handed it to me. He offered me the menu and asked if I was hungry, what could he bring me? I took a quick peek and said a little pizza and a good pinot noir. He said he would be right back and told me to take a few minutes to unpack. I did as he said.

He returned and placed the tray on the table, opened the door to the balcony, and handed me a blanket. He said, "You have a lovely view, even at night. Go ahead, the blanket will keep you warm." I grabbed my journal, sat in the chair, and stared out into the black night. He brought me a glass of wine and handed me a plate with a slice of pizza. He asked if I needed anything else. I said no. Thank you. What do I need to sign? I got up to give him a tip. He said, "You stay there. I'll be around. I promise, you will be fine, you have found the right place. Get some rest."

I took a big gulp of wine, opened the journal, looked out into the pitch black night, and thought it was just like my life, black. "How appropriate." I don't think I was ever able to tell someone, including myself, what I wanted from life. I started writing and this is what showed up:

- How do I clarify my life's purpose? Why am I here?
- Where is my "home" – that place of calm and serene, where I feel balance, security, life?
- How do I find an appropriate, responsible role and balance for my work and personal lives? Can I live a life that separates the two?

- What are my life's goals beyond work? Why don't I have any or any that I spend any real time pursuing?
- How do I balance the seemingly unending "neediness" of the people in my life? How do I assert myself and where's my real accountability?
- How will I find love if I can't unprotect my heart, let it breathe, take that chance with the hope that I find the one who deserves it?

I read it and re-read it – not sure where the words came from but sure the pen in my hand was in motion. The last one, it had a powerful force field around it and came from an unknown place within me. Love? Really? I had sworn off love, convinced it couldn't be a part of me. My ego had told me many times that I was not worthy of love. My heart was shattered. I didn't deserve love; I wasn't worthy of love.

As I looked out at the sky, my eyes adjusted to the darkness, and I started to see something. Tiny lights in the sky, stars. They had been there the whole time, I just hadn't seen them until this moment. There's always light in the darkness, always. You just have to look for it. Remember? Chicago? I realized love is what I wanted, perhaps most of all. A small inner voice deep inside me was finally heard. It broke through all the walls, all the anger; it emerged from the darkness of the castle to tell me that love was indeed what I sought.

The next morning, I stopped at the front desk to leave a tip for the bellman. I asked for the front desk manager and explained I wanted to be sure this note got to him, he had been quite helpful and kind last night; he was a wonderful person. The manager looked at me a little sideways. He said, "Last night? Ms. Nagel, you arrived last evening?" I said "Yes, around 9 pm." He said, "And he said his name was Ben?" I said, "Yes, I'm pretty sure that's what he told me." I described him. He said, "I'm sorry Ms. Nagel. I've been on duty since you checked in. There was no bell service last night. The regular guy was off sick and there is no one working here named Ben. I have no idea who helped you last night. Must have been a guardian angel. " He laughed. I looked at him, he looked at me and I smiled.

Standing on a New Edge

Before I left Durham, I made arrangements to take a private hike and explore the vortex energies known to be strong in Sedona. I selected a guide who was Native American and accessed her intuitive gifts to help others discover what was keeping them from their life's aspirations.

I was excited as I set off to meet her. I had everything I could possibly need in my pack. I tried to prepare for any situation no matter how big or small. Talk about a metaphor for my life. In truth, I was totally unprepared for the challenge that was upon me. There wasn't a band-aid, antacid, saline spray, sunscreen, or ibuprofen tablet that was going to help me.

The guide took me on a unique hike up Cathedral Rock. She had located seven vortex zones and associated these to each of the body's chakra energy zones. In Sanskrit, chakra means vortex and Sedona is known to have some of the most powerful vortexes on earth.[3] This hike and concept tied to the work I had started with Jenna Rae a few years earlier. I was intrigued. As we moved through the chakra zones, we explored my life, searched for my intentions, and unearthed what impeded me from experiencing joy in my life. She blended her intuitive and empathic gifts with her Native American heritage, ceremony, and medicine to reach deeper into my energy field and help me find resolve and release. As she gently guided me along the trail and discussed impediments, I slowly came to realize that I was perhaps one of the biggest blocks to my own happiness.

We started our journey in root chakra. It's the foundation of our self: family, beliefs, safety, instinct, and boundaries. Blockages in root chakra often originate from old family wounds and disruptions and trauma experienced during childhood. I placed immediate focus on my family and the traumatic parts of my childhood that I recalled. I touched on my repressed memories and the nightmares. We talked about the estrangement from my brother, and the ongoing complications with my mother. I could have spent all day in this chakra zone, but there was more work ahead of me.

Sacral energy focuses on the flow of life and is controlled by fears and inability to trust. Among the associated body parts are your lower back, sexual organs, and digestion. The endometriosis was a *physical* manifestation of my sacral blockages. I had hoped that an upcoming small surgical procedure would help clear the physical pain and allow me to begin clearing this energy. I had no idea at this point how much work would be needed here. We kept walking.

The next energy was solar plexus and it became difficult for me to move and breathe as we approached. Solar plexus is the personal power zone, often considered the ego and identity. Solar plexus drives confidence, responsibility, willpower and self-discipline. It helps meet challenges as we move forward in life. I walked into the epicenter of my being and I was suffocating. I blamed the altitude, but it had nothing to do with that. I shared how difficult it had always been for me to find the right balance for work and how survival was an instinct for me as a result of the trauma in my life. I could feel my protector managing the situation, to keep things covered as I was trying to release a part of this to the world. I was battling with my own ego to be honest with myself.

We moved into heart chakra. I thought this part of the hike would kill me. Heart chakra is the place where love, compassion, and feelings of self-love and respect emanate. It conveys the sense of wholeness and recognizes our context within and extension into the universe. It's the heart that has the ultimate capacity and strength to heal. My heart pounded and beat strongly and quickly that I couldn't get it under control. It was my heart pounding on my ego. It was sending a clear message of its ability. We came upon this most beautiful juniper growing out to the rock with a graceful twisted trunk. I cried when I saw this tree. I could hardly breathe; my heart pounding and I grabbed hold of one of the branches. The guide told me to close my eyes, take some deep breaths, lean into the earth's energy, and specifically experience what this tree offered me. In this moment, a new world opened up to me.

It was the first time I saw her, me, as the seven-year-old. She was a flash in my mind, but I could *feel her*, she was living in my heart. She was sad and afraid, but willing. It was that moment I realized who and what I had shut down years ago. She was here to show me as an adult what I needed to see in a new light. My entire aura was awash in this lavender light field, and I was attached to this tree in an electromagnetic sense that caused no pain. As I drew each breath up from the earth, I could feel the love come into my body, my toes, fingers, blood. It was a steady and gentle release of tension.

I don't know how long I stayed like that, and I heard the guide's quiet voice ask me how I was feeling. I told her I wasn't sure, I wasn't in pain, but I was definitely feeling a little dizzy, loopy in a good way. The energy was amazing. She smiled and said it probably felt good for me to feel my heart. My heart and ego were at war. My ego was a bully strangling my heart and trying to consume the space they both held. As I listened and held onto that tree, I heard what I long knew, but no one had ever told me in quite this way. My ego had become a *tyrant*. I was here to figure out how to wage battle with it. I didn't have the first clue what to do with it, but I understood.

We moved onward and upward into throat chakra. The air got a little thinner. My heart was pounding hard, and it felt like it was in my throat. I thought I was going to throw up. I could only take a few steps at a time.

It was here that I started to see the next major issue ahead of me. Throat chakra helps us with communication and expression. It is also the chakra zone where anger ultimately leaves us. Well, I had always had challenges communicating my emotions, feelings, and anger. I had grown up being told my emotions didn't matter and no one wanted to hear how I felt. Therapy softened this sensation somewhat, but it was still a significant struggle. She asked if I wanted to stop and turn back. Nope, there was no turning back. I would make it all the way to the top. This was what I was supposed to do. I was meant to be there and I may puke ten times, but I'll make it. We pushed onward.

As we stretched into third eye, the wind picked up strength and began to gust. The third eye chakra is located between your eyes and it allows us to see a deeper perspective in this world as well as other dimensions and realms. It provides clear thought and the opportunity for spiritual contemplation and guidance. It was the place where my intuitive gifts first appeared after decades in hiding. The wind whipped around us at a dangerous velocity. Yet, it wasn't pushing us off the cliff. Instead, it felt like it was blowing through us. I felt a clearing, a cleansing. I thought of a scene from Forrest Gump, the one where Lt. Dan is on the boat in the middle of a hurricane. He's hanging atop the mast pole and screaming at the heavens to come get him if they want him, but he wasn't going without a fight. The guide and I took hold of a tree and held on as the wind whipped through us. I made a prayer. If my life was going to end, then come and get me, and end it, now. Take me out. I was ready; and if this wasn't my time, then enough is enough. Let's figure out exactly what I'm supposed to be doing here in this world. I had major blockages in five chakra zones. I'll do the work. Help me.

It was too dangerous to hike into crown chakra. As we hiked down the rock, I began to feel the energy, the essence of the spirit in this land. It was here to heal, to protect, to help. I wasn't sure where I would go, but the message was clear. It was not time for me to go permanently, it was time for me to stay, and it was time for me to become what I had always wanted. I didn't know what that meant, but I knew somehow it would be okay. This was the first of almost twenty hikes and I would take up Cathedral Rock in the course of the next five years.

Back at the hotel, I slept the soundest sleep I had ever known. No demons, no monsters. At breakfast, I heard the waiter talking to another guest about the windstorm. Weirdest thing. It had been something like a hundred years since Sedona had experienced a wind as intense as what blew in yesterday. The gusts were almost hurricane strength and he knew; he was from the east coast. It was a freakish phenomenon. He had no idea how anyone got any sleep last night with all that wind.

There are some who consider the wind to be a living being in and of itself, a God capable of communicating a language to those who may hear it if we open ourselves to the messages it brings. Some Native Americans consider the wind to be a divine messenger. It seeks unity, balance, harmony, and freedom. This wind, it was there to listen to my heart and to tell me, that I was on the right path and it was time to pay attention.

I also spent some time on this trip with a Native American elder. She shared her wisdom with respect to Native American spirituality and tradition. The wind was my element. I should not be afraid that I could see the wind, it was a powerful ally to me, and she would teach me how to use it. She introduced me to the medicine of the brown bear. The bear symbolizes strength, confidence, and the heart. When the bear comes, it's time for healing and specifically, healing of the heart. The bear represents the importance of solitude and rest as evidenced by their hibernation. Awake, they roam the earth peacefully and without aggression, yet have the capacity to be a great warrior when taunted or challenged. The bear became my medicine. It was time to call upon the bear to show my heart the way to rest, heal, strengthen, and live in the world as a peaceful warrior.[4] It was time to live first from heart and not my ego.

I left Sedona knowing that I had made progress. My journey would be long and I had no real idea when or what might happen next, but I had found my spiritual essence. I found my healing space and safe haven. In the months that followed, I reflected on my experiences. I worked on my lessons and "homework" from my hike. I made plans to return in a few months. My spiritual self was wide-awake and ready to learn, explore, and resolve the mess that was me.

December 31, 2009

Back home I was at the tip of a frightening reality, and preparing for a battle I had no idea was coming. Over the next months, tensions between my partner and I escalated. We continued to have differences regarding deadlines and commitments. We had several arguments and unproductive, hurtful moments on both sides. They say it takes two to tango, and it seemed we were doing a good job at that. It was a new, disturbing pattern to our relationship. We were disagreeing, landing differently, and losing our middle ground.

We reached the beginning of our end on December 31, 2009. My partner left a message saying he needed to speak with me. I was enjoying time away from work with my teenage nieces. I was miffed that I was being called away from personal time; I had become much better at breaking from work in the months that followed my first trip to Sedona. He seemed insistent and I called when I had a moment.

What transpired next was an unexpected argument. He had questions regarding selected financial statements related to year-end performance. Financials and "the books" were in my domain and I was perplexed. We both had equal access to the company financials. I was hearing him question the integrity of certain actions. I heard accusations that I had been keeping things from him and was stealing from the company. I heard him tell me he didn't believe that I was being truthful, and I exploded.

There was yelling and screaming. I was not about to lose this battle, and I sensed equal fight. I was defending my honor with the full capacity of my arsenal. I would not be defeated and my integrity would not be questioned under any circumstance.

When I slammed down the phone, I was shaking. My anger was immense. I saw my nieces staring at me. They had been waiting for me in the other room, and they had never seen me angry. They were frightened and worried. I could see they didn't know how to react at first. I told them that I was extremely angry. This had nothing to do with them. I needed a favor and made them a promise. We got in the car to pick up some things for the New Year's party. I needed to vent a bit. I promised them this venting would last as long as we were in the car. I didn't need them to do anything except let me talk. As soon as we got home and slammed the car doors shut, it would be finished. We would get back to having fun. I kept that promise.

It was December 31, 2009. It was the thirty-fifth anniversary of my father's passing, and it seemed another end was now upon me.

A New Year, A New Choice

On New Year's Day, I sat at the table with my friends and we picked up our conversation from the year before. I shared with them the realization that I had come to just the day before. The business I had founded and built, and the relationship with my business partner was ending. At that table, I had not the first clue of how or when it would ultimately end. I only knew it would. I knew significant change was upon me, and I was terrified. I sat there and tried to figure out who I was, what I would be, how I would live if I didn't have my business. I pondered why, on the same day I lost my innocence as a child, this traumatic event landed in my lap.

My nieces and friends were of great comfort. We spent hours talking and they helped me find laughter amidst my fear, and assured me of the love and support they were all ready to provide. The next morning I dropped the girls at the airport. I sat in the parking lot for a long time. I didn't want to go home because I knew home meant reality. I needed to face the situation with my business. I needed to face the situation with my life. Eventually, I turned the key and started my way home. I pulled into the garage, sat on the couch, and cried for a long time.

I considered the possibility that there was a different option. I considered everything I had learned in my time in Sedona. I recalled the lesson of the bear and how the bear had shown up to protect me when I was challenged. I wondered what it was that I actually wanted. I knew my protector was ready to step in and make war. What did my heart want? What was the purpose for this happening on the anniversary of my father's death? The day my life changed forever because of the actions and will of others. Was I now being called to willfully and intentionally change my life in light of my own goals and desires?

I drew a hot bubble bath and poured a big glass of wine. I lit the candles and settled in for a good soak. In the quiet, dark calm I melted into the heat of the water and the calming vanilla and sandalwood. I pondered these questions. Was this an opportunity wrapped in an ugly mask? Could I shift my perception to see this not as a burden or something that had been done to me? I had spent many years wondering the "why." What would it be like if I started to ask myself, "For what purpose does this serve me?" If I could allow myself to accept that another direction was possible, could I allow myself to accept then this was not something thrown in my face to hurt me? This was being given to me to help me find my way back to the heart and that little girl. Was this my light in the darkness?

I took a deep breath and made my choice. I would take the fear of ending something that was centric to my being and use it as a gift, an opportunity to learn, grow, and begin anew. I would figure out what I wanted from life, and then I would figure out how to create that life. At this moment, I chose *me*. I was terrified as a new, stronger, intentional voice emerged within me.

PART FOUR

Untethered

Me, the **adult** heart ... to the protector.

Albert Einstein said,

"Try not to become a man of success, but rather try to become a man of value.[5]"

I bring Albert Einstein to your attention for three important reasons. He is one of the most brilliant minds in history. He saw the relationship between elements seen and unseen. He believed in love and heart, and that it mattered in everything.

I'm going to take a shot here and guess what you are thinking. You need a plan, a big one, a plan that will allow you to do battle and win. You are ready to dig deep into your arsenal and I can see the battle plan sketching out on the whiteboard. I bet you believe this is the battle you have trained our whole life for and you are ready to do whatever you have to do to win.

Yeah, we aren't going to do that. I have a different plan. I think it's time we start working together. Let me say first *that I'm grateful for everything you have done. You stepped in when I needed you most. You stepped up, you provided. You got it done. I'm not going to say it was always pretty, but we are still standing, and that is due in large part to your work.*

I've grown up. No longer the heart of a little girl but one of grown woman with a fresh resolve. I found that seven-year-old little girl in my heart in Sedona. I also found me in Sedona, the grown up heart of that little girl ready to figure out how to beat strong.

We are going to do the best we can to stop living a life based upon surviving, coping, and reacting to what's thrown at us. I have no idea how we will do this. We will stumble. We will fall, and there will be times the fall will hurt. We have no idea how much this may hurt. We will listen to the heart first, and then use our mind with our heart to help craft the path to brilliance and joy.

This business is done. I don't know when or how or in what form, but it's done. I'll say this to your battle plans. There will be no war. There may be anger and there may be a need to defend what's fair and just, but we will not make war. We play fair. We keep playing fair. If someone chooses a different tact, we still play fair.

We are going to lose something we worked extremely hard to create, our identity. You had the heavier hand in creating it, and I'm responsible for taking a back seat and letting you drive the bus. I admit I took comfort in your process. It allowed me to shelter my pain. Now we must work together. While I have no idea how we will do this, there are some promises I'm willing to make on our behalf.

First, we are going to be honest with ourselves. We are going to see the truth - good and bad - for we are made of both. We are going to figure out what works and what will not in our new world order. If it doesn't work, then we do whatever we need to shift it. This is about letting go of what no longer serves in the hope that we create a space for something new.

Second, we will be committed to our goal. This heart pounds with fear, but probably not in the way you might think. My fear is what will happen if we don't change. Taking a chance on change is less risky compared to continuing a life as we are. There will be times when we will want to quit and revert back to our old ways. During those times, you will need to lean heavily upon me and listen to how strong and capable I have become. In the end, I promise it will be me, not you that will see us through.

Third, we will find moments to laugh, no matter what. We will search for humor in the darkest moments, toughest battles, and biggest adversities. It will make the bad, dark and ugly less so. I believe that laughter tells us that no matter what, we will be all right. And we are going to be all right.

We will find what we need along the way. In this I trust and believe. Trust is something we don't have a lot of experience with, and this will be a big challenge. It may be something we are challenged to achieve for the rest of our lives, and we will keep trying. We will trust in ourselves first, and then trust in others who have been brought here to help guide, support, and love us through our journey.

How will we do this? We will remember the moments we were about to jump off the swings. The moment we decided it was time to jump. The moment we flew. When we didn't know if we would land or fall, and we didn't care, because we were flying. In those moments, you and I are working in perfect harmony. We gave the little girl will to risk and courage to leap. We allowed her the possibility of the fall, thrill in the landing, and joy that knowing no matter what, she flew.

You see, it's our turn. It's our turn to make new choices.

CHAPTER THIRTEEN

Finding the Heart

These were the first steps of what would become an almost five-year journey. My first challenge was to get a grip on exactly what it was that I promised myself I would do. I made a commitment to myself to do things differently. I was asking myself to enter into an ongoing negotiation between my ego and heart, to find a common ground and emerge into the world as a peaceful warrior, not a fierce protector.

Darwin (Again)

I had to face the challenges of my business. It supported my life, and provided for my well-being. It also brought me an interesting challenge. I couldn't run. This wasn't a job, it was a company. I had responsibilities and obligations. I had to address every aspect of what led me to this point and determine the best course going forward. I wasn't alone in this. I was in a marriage of sorts with my partner and we had a big house, in this case, our technology, and children in the form of clients. Up until that day in December, I trusted him implicitly and believed he trusted me. I was confident that we acted based upon the best interests of each other. This may have been true and true even in this moment; yet, it was invisible and hidden under anger, confusion, and shock. His challenge to my integrity hurt me deeply. This created a compulsion to fight and prove I was right.

I hadn't done anything wrong, and I wasn't lying. I was shocked because he was the last person that I thought would ever question my integrity.

The conflict within me was that I didn't want to fight him. The protector within me was heading to the war room drawing plans. The heart within me was hurt that I hadn't been believed and that I had said things to a person I loved that were unkind. I needed to protect and defend myself and my rights as co-owner of this business, but I needed a sense of fairness that was allowing my heart to be heard and balanced with my protector. I kept asking myself, "What am I supposed to learn from this?"

I found the lesson in the days following our argument. We went round and round on issues and couldn't move. It seemed to me that we had landed in two different places and neither one of us was willing to budge. We lost trust in each other, and this was breaking our relationship apart. In listening to my partner, I started seeing how he was seeing me. I was seeing myself through my heart; I was loving, caring, and nurturing. I would never do anything to intentionally hurt him. I was seeing myself as I *wanted* to be seen. My sense was that my partner was seeing me as I was *really* showing up in the world. I was showing up ready for battle; guarded, defensive, and prepared to prove my point until my opponent relented and retreated.

I became a survivor at the age of seven and honed those protective skills in the years following my father's death. Survival had become instinct to me. Not the basic food, clothing, and shelter need for survival, the survival that was ready for the fight and prepared to win at all costs. Winning did not mean you beat someone at something, it meant you were still alive. I was showing up as a force to be reckoned, tough, guarded, and right. It was crucially important to be believed and he didn't believe me in this moment. I was going to have to tear all of this apart.

I realized if I wanted to approach this as the peaceful warrior and *not* the grizzly bear, I was going to have to change my inherent nature to survive. I needed to deconstruct everything my protector had built. How do I do that? I was about to find out. I was going to have to unlearn how to lead from a place of *protect and defend* and learn how to use my heart and allow the caring part of me to come forward. I needed to unlearn reaction from fear, and learn how to live in strength. I needed to unlearn how to listen and react through my mind and start hearing and trusting my heart. This was the crux of my issue. The battle between my heart, the protector and the adult persona I manifested from this energy within me, my ego. I wanted to be seen as I saw myself, and in order to do that, I had to teach my ego to stand down. Was there a place on the other "side" of the survival instinct? What was it like? What would it be like if I could get there?

From my perspective, we were operating without the element of trust. What changed? I wasn't convinced it was center on this one instance. I was seeing this as the trigger to something that had been building for a long time. Our circumstances changed. What we wanted for our lives evolved and we were either going to adapt or become extinct. It seemed that over time we became less driven by the goals of the business and more driven by what we needed and expected from the business. I was realizing what we expected from each other had changed as well. For years, these needs and expectation had been close enough. Now, it seemed there was a gap and it was widening. I thought back upon the conversation I had before I took the job in Chicago. The Darwin experiment. Things were going to change and it was completely possible that some might not survive and this wasn't bad, this was evolution. The natural order of things. I started to realize there was no right or wrong in this situation. There just *was* this situation, and it needed to be managed delicately. We had clients, technology, and obligations to honor and support. We had a relationship that had been solid and trusting. There was no "cut and run" this time; I would create a deliberate path.

I asked myself, what would happen if I lost everything with the business right then? What would my life be like if it all went away in a puff of smoke? Would I be okay? What would I do? How would I survive? I needed a plan. I didn't put a war plan together to battle my partner. I put contingency plans in place so I felt safe knowing that if something catastrophic happened, I had an idea of how I would get through it. I used these plans as my source of comfort as my partner and I tried to find a common ground.

Finally, I needed a sense of fairness in everything we did. When anger flared between us (and it did, especially in those early days), I tried my best to see my partner's perspective and find a common ground based on what seemed respectful to us both. It was not easy and I failed miserably at first, but in time I started to get it. I came to know some things with respect to my partner's commitments to the business that were upsetting to me. I created a file that I dubbed the "box of ugly." It was a spot where I parked all of these upsetting findings. The goal was to never touch it. As soon as I did, the matters between us would become unpleasant, combative, and irreconcilable. I reminded myself constantly of my goal. Play fair and even if he didn't play fair, keep playing fair, it's who I am. It would set me free.

We agreed that we would set our differences aside and honor Rule Number One – the client was first and their best interests were our priority. We hired a consultant, a "marriage counselor" of sorts, who helped mediate our differences and re-build a semblance of trust in our relationship. We continued to argue and vented years of frustration that seemed pent up within us. We were reminded that we had built a great business together and our relationship had held tight for a long time. The fact that we had made it this far without conflict was a significant accomplishment in any business partnership. The challenge was that our relationship was changing and we wanted different things. Whether it was one incident or many, we weren't the same people to each other anymore. Eventually, we found a cadence, a safe operating mode. As we grew steadier in this space, we started to have real conversations regarding our options. We agreed it was time to look at ways to exit. We were in the stages of a divorce. It was amicable at the moment, but we were getting unhitched, nonetheless. We would become extinct.

Working on the Heart

I made four trips to Sedona in 2010 and each trip brought broader perspective, deeper understanding and fueled the desire to keep learning. I used Sedona as an immersion program to identify and deconstruct the parts of me that no longer served who I was and what I wanted to be. Sedona was going to be the place where I would learn how to change my instinct. Therapy had taught me how I became the way I was. Now, it was up to me to figure out how to become the person that lived outside the protective barriers of the survivor's instinct. My ego was the gatekeeper and it was drowning and choking the real power of my soul, my heart. I had seen my heart to know it was possible to live from a place of love. The protector was an invisible force field around me and she was strong and not willing to listen at first. She assumed she knew what was best under any circumstance, and that was about to change.

I found my spiritual grounding in Sedona. I began each visit at The Chapel of the Holy Cross. It's a beautiful representation of how traditional religious practice meets the greater spiritual perspective that comes from the land and its ancestors. For me, it became the place where balance came into my awareness. I was raised in the Methodist church yet I was a not a person of structured religion. In the years before I came to Sedona, I studied Eastern and Western religion and philosophy. In Sedona, I added the dimension of Native American spirituality and medicine. I learned and practiced Native ceremony in all of my work. I explored these beliefs along with other Eastern and Western philosophies and concepts. In time, I blended these and created a solid foundation based on my own spiritual beliefs.

As you approach the Chapel, there is a rock formation that many call the "spirit wall." As you look at the rock formation, it's possible to see the shapes of faces in the rock. Many believe these are the spirits of the land coming to bless you with gifts and guidance. Inside this small Catholic chapel there are flanks of candles and the front window provides you a beautiful view of Cathedral Rock. I connected into the essence of Sedona at the Chapel, prayed for guidance and wisdom, and expressed gratitude for the blessings of the ancestors, the spirits and the land. I listened to my inner spirit during those moments and formulated the "agenda" for my work during each particular trip. The Chapel also was the place where I could connect strongly with my dad, and I could feel his presence and hear him speak to me.

Each visit to Sedona included a hike up Cathedral Rock. I waged a peaceful, deliberate battle against my solar plexus chakra (where the ego and protector lived), allowing it to be strong, but teaching it to open up and listen to my heart. This would be a slow, evolutionary process as I allowed my heart to find light and asked my ego to shift ever so slowly into the shadow. The first outer barriers were quite tough and resistant to change, but I kept at it. In time, I started to feel a stronger sense of equilibrium.

Each hike unearthed another dimension or layer of myself that was ready to be addressed. As something new revealed itself to me, I focused and created as much awareness around the one issue, attribute, habit, behavior, or situation. I reflected upon it to understand how, where, and to what extent it played in my life. I searched to understand for what purpose it had served, was serving at the moment, and might serve in my life going forward. In therapy, much of my work took place in the "chair" and my time for reflection was after. In Sedona, there was an aspect to this work that was tacit. I was hiking, moving, creating, and exploring; there was a physical aspect to the emotional and spiritual shifting and somehow this resonated within me in a way that compelled me forward.

I merged the physical, emotional, and spiritual dimensions within me to motivate and drive change.

Sedona became the place where I allowed my heart to roam freely. I felt such safety there and this led me to slowly allow those loving, caring aspects of my personality (my heart) that had been in the darkness find their way to the light. Sedona allowed me to be what I wanted to be. I was able to play and explore life without the structure and constraint of the "professional" self. An inner hippie emerged and I loved to drop into the new mellow, open energy. I let it all go and allowed the softer side of me to emerge. In doing so, I became even more acquainted with my heart and let the seven-year-old out to play. At the end of those first trips, I "packed up" the heart and the hippie, and kept them safe until next time. In time, I became more comfortable and confident allowing both out into the greater world outside Sedona. It was met with huge, positive support from people in every aspect of my life, professional and personal. I found another thing when I was searching for my heart in Sedona. I found hearts – actual hearts. It started with heart-shaped rocks as I hiked along the trails in Sedona. Then, I started finding them everywhere I went. The more I released the heart and inner hippie within me, the more I found hearts *everywhere*. It was an amazing reminder and motivating symbol to keep me going.

I left Sedona with "homework" to take back into the real world. I used that time between visits to practice and learn. I was creating awareness around what I was trying to change within myself. I stumbled and fell as I made changes. In time, I found the falls got softer and lighter the more I focused on *what* I was learning about myself in the process as opposed to the sting that can come with the fall.

I created awareness as a strong sense of honesty about myself. I learned to see the good, bad, and ugly that lived within me. I began to resolve inner conflicts. I made a mental list of what I was going to change, the new behaviors I wanted to encourage, evaluated which old habits I needed to release, and which barriers should be dropped. I was learning and in doing so, had to accept that it would take some time. The process required patience and I had never been a patient person. Great patience was required with my memory recovery. Now, it extended out into every aspect of my life, as I used what I was learning to up-end and transform. I got frustrated. I ran into myself all the time. I had to *accept and trust* that the universe had its own timetable. I could continue to do my work and at the right time and moment, the result, the benefit of the work would appear. Until then, I stayed in practice, maintained awareness, and accepted the process for what it was.

My work in Sedona was different from therapy. I wouldn't have been successful there had I not been through a therapeutic process first. Therapy provided a scaffold upon which to hang all of the things that happened to me. It taught me how those events lived within me. Sedona was teaching me what options I had to make other choices. Who did I want to become as a result of what I now understood? I created a new dimension to my persona in Sedona, the spiritual one. I was finding a strong sense of higher purpose in the world. I remembered the conversation I had with Jenna Rae three years earlier, when she told me there would be a time to live more fully into my spiritual calling. It was time.

A Writer Emerges

I also discovered something else the more I worked on myself. I started writing and I loved it. I took great comfort in the blank page. It invited me to fill it with all the things I was thinking, questions I wanted to explore, and emotions I needed to feel or understand. Writing became a way in which I could expose myself, my true self, to *me*. In the beginning, I caught the protector within me, shielding me from my true feelings. I was trying to structure my writing in a way that my professional or ego would like it to be. It felt like I was creating something for a client. I had to detach myself from the belief that it always had to be perfect. The truth was, the less perfect, the better. It meant I was out of my head and into my heart. Writing became a mechanism for me to engage with my heart's true voice. I allowed myself to use the space to explore, learn, and let go.

I began writing letters. If I was working on an issue that involved someone, I wrote a letter and told them everything I was feeling. If it was something regarding me, I might write a letter to myself and then use that letter to dive deeper into my emotions and remain in a curious state. I learned more about me. I was always safe in my writing, and I could explore the full context of my feelings. I could be completely and brutally honest in my words. My emotions mattered if only on this page in the moment I was writing them. Overtime, writing quieted that inner voice that told me my emotions didn't matter. I was slowly learning to allow my emotional self to emerge and in time, share it with others. Writing became the way I taught myself how to express emotion and feeling.

Letter writing became a huge, cathartic tool. I learned how to release and let go through writing. Many issues involved people who were not alive or present to listen to what I was saying. I had to find my own sense of resolve. I wrote a letter, spoke my mind, found my peace, and then let go. Part of letting go usually included holding a match to that letter and burning it. There was an amazing sense of freedom that came with watching those letters go up in flames.

New Year's Check-in

On New Year's Day in 2011, I gathered with my friends and nieces and served my feast. We toasted the gifts of friendship and love and progress made since our last meeting at this New Year's table. We pondered our upcoming year and made our wishes and predictions and agreed to reconvene next year. My friends commented on how much more peaceful I seemed sitting at the table. They could tell I was still confused, but I was *happier*. As I cleaned up that night and the girls wandered off to bed, I wondered to myself how the next year would unfold. I drew a hot bubble bath and poured one last glass of wine. The past year had brought significant change and growth. What treasures might this coming year hold for me? What more would I learn and how much more would I change as a result? I drank in the familiar scents of vanilla and sandalwood, and realized there was a lot of unknown ahead of me. I was afraid, but far less so compared to a year ago. My perspective was broader, deeper, and richer. I was less concerned with thoughts of what *would* ultimately happen and more curious contemplating what *might* happen along the way. I toasted myself with that last sip of wine to the continued adventure that was my life.

CHAPTER FOURTEEN

Finding Health

The year started with a flurry of activity surrounding efforts to sell the business. We were finding that some of our options were falling away and new ones emerging. It was slower paced than what we had been told by some advisors, and this was discouraging. We weren't defeated, but started the year re-setting some expectations.

The Last Stop

The pain from my endometriosis returned and it appeared that the disease had won the war. I was on the last stop of this long journey. There was no other option; it was time for a hysterectomy. I was forty-four and felt a strange sense of relief as I sat in my doctor's office and discussed the procedure and possible outcomes. It was almost anti-climactic. I had lost my ability to have children more than a decade before. I was playing a waiting game, and it had come to an end. The feeling I had was one of relief and hope that I might finally be free from pain, drug treatments, and the uncertainty that goes with disease.

From a practical perspective, I needed a couple of months to prepare for the surgery and post-operation recovery. There would be no work: no laptop, no cell phone, no email for at least a week, possibly longer. A restricted schedule would last another eight to ten weeks, depending on my healing. I needed rest and a low stress environment. My partner was tremendously supportive when I told him. He told me to have the surgery as soon as I wanted. I felt the essence of our old relationship. We put a plan together and I felt compassion and support from him. It would be the first time since I started the business that I was not allowed to work at all. It was about letting go of my need to always be available. I needed to take care of me.

Spiritual Perspective

I went to Sedona a couple of weeks before my surgery and took my hike up Cathedral Rock. I spent a great deal of time working with root and sacral chakra energy in preparation for this surgery. This wasn't physical; my mind centered upon the long emotional journey I had experienced with this disease and what it cost me. The "root chakra" part of this hike involves a couple of huge trees that lean and bend into each other. They were described to me as the family trees and they are a fitting representation of root chakra.

There is one that seems to allow me to lean on it, like two people would lean back to back. One of the trunks is the perfect "back" to mine. I love the view from this vantage point. There is a small creek that runs off the much larger Oak Creek. That little side creek has its own small waterfalls and trickling water. It branches off in an arc and then rejoins the creek further down the path. I climbed into the tree and leaned into its back. That's when I saw it; a stroller parked by the creek; someone had left it there. I looked at it a long time. I watched the water rush past it as it sat gently by the side. The current seemed strong even on this tiny stream and I felt a sense of cleansing, purifying, as I watched the water pass. It had been sixteen years since my first surgery. Since that day I sat on the couch and grieved with the mothers in Oklahoma City who lost children. It had been a long journey, and it was ending.

My mind drifted to all sorts of places, past and present. I wondered what it would have been like had the endometriosis never happened. I prayed to allow this to be the end to the pain and disease. I asked for strength and support as I healed. I prayed for the children I would never know and asked that they be loved, wherever they were. I stayed in that tree for a long time and watched the water flow. Something was shifting in me. I felt no rush to move on to anything else. I was content in the stillness and the permission I gave myself to reflect. I was in a peaceful mind and heart before I left the tree and moved onward with the hike and my life.

A New To-Do-List

I arrived back home and prepared for surgery. I had this massive "to do" list for both work and personal. I wanted to have as much completed to eliminate worry about tasks and chores while I was recovering. I was fearful of the unknown road ahead. I had no idea how my body was going to react to the surgery or what my life would be after. The pain I experienced just prior to seemed to reach a crescendo, as if to send one last cannonball into the battleground. I felt miserable as I plowed through this list. It seemed like I just kept adding things to it. There was no end in sight, and yet there had to be an end. I was going into surgery and would have to be unplugged for at least a week. There was a hard stop to my life. I looked at the huge list of all of the things I needed to accomplish before I shut down and walked away. Yet, all I wanted to do was rest. I was tired. My life was on the verge of a significant change. As strange as it seemed, I was used to a life of physical ups and downs. The pain, the limitations, the seemingly never-ending chaos that I experienced with this disease and treatment had been a constant focal point for decades. I was a little nervous about what life might be like without pain.

I looked back at the list, and I realized something. In my last few hours before this major life event, how was I going to spend my time? Was I going to run the clock down trying to get every possible thing for work completed? What was the worst thing that could happen? I looked at my list, my desk, and my computer. I put the list off to the side; I changed my auto reply on email and updated my voicemail message. I turned off my computer and straightened up my desk. I pulled the doors to the office shut and went downstairs. I sat outside in the afternoon sun and meditated. I contemplated, I hoped this would be the last day I lived in pain. I *celebrated* that I chose me, and what was best for me personally in this moment.

The surgery was complicated and lasted almost four hours. I had difficulties waking from the anesthesia. In my hospital room, my doctor pulled up a chair and took my hand. She told me that in all of her years practicing she had never seen a case quite as severe as mine. I was a true example of how vicious this disease could be. It had been particularly evil to me.

She also told me that she wasn't entirely certain she understood how I had been functioning. The physical pain should have been substantial and debilitating. What my body had withstood had taken a toll; there had been considerable damage. How long had I been in such pain? I told her simply, a long time, but I had made incremental adjustments to it to the point I was finally able to block it out. She was concerned and shook her head a little. Recovery would take longer than we had anticipated. She was benching me from all work for the next couple of weeks. I had one job at the moment, and that was to rest as much as possible.

The doctor said, "Kate, I'm concerned that you could be hurt and you wouldn't even know it because you are used to managing your pain within yourself." I nodded and started crying. She had no idea how correct she was in that statement. She gave me a hug. As she left the room, she turned, smiled softly, and said, "Here's what I'll say about all of this. With all of the anesthesia and pain meds, you should be a little more out of it than you are. But your eyes are clear, and you know exactly what's happening. I can see that you are better already. The worst is behind you. Get some rest. Lots and lots of rest. Promise me." I nodded yes, I promise.

I spent the summer on the couch and followed doctor's orders. I was not allowed to lift anything heavier than a gallon of milk. I had people in to help me for weeks. She was right that my body would tell me to stop, and I listened. The anesthesia left my mind a little wobbly. It was nearly impossible for me to concentrate on anything. My short-term memory was spotty, and it was a couple weeks before I could spend more than a few minutes writing in my journal. I took nice slow walks. I slept and slept and slept. Every day, I felt a little stronger and more capable. Every day, more of the impact of that disease left my body.

Almost ten weeks later, my doctor released me, and she set me free to go about the world. I had the physicality and health profile of a woman in her twenties, not forties, and I should keep up the good work. As I left her office, I handed her a small piece of garnet. It was a stone that represented my root chakra element, and I had carried it with me for the past few years. I kept it with me through my surgery and recovery and now I was giving it to her. I had thought the disease had won the war, but it appears *I* had won, with her help. I wanted her to have the garnet because she was the one who helped me clear this disease from my body. I thanked her for saving my life. Every time I see her, she lets me know she still has that garnet stone.

I started running again, and I reveled in my ability to move without pain. I was physically free for the first time in almost thirty years. In October, I committed with a group of friends to train for my first half marathon the following spring.

Tensions Building

I spent the remainder of 2011 working on exit opportunities for the business. We learned the process was not easy and we were not sure how long it would last. We were holding on and doing the best we could, but I could sense frustration building with the process and with each other.

New Year Check-in

On New Year's Day, I welcomed my friends to my home for a feast. That year my nieces weren't there. They were teenage girls tangled up in boys, friends, and part-time jobs so they stayed home for the holiday. We again sat at the table and again checked in on our progress with our goals, hopes, and dreams. I felt as if I were a completely different person. The surgery had caused a major physical transformation; I had energy, strength and endurance like I had never felt. The business was becoming increasingly frustrating, and I wasn't sure how much longer we could hold on. Yet my value for the business had shifted. The surgery and my extended recovery had shown me the power of rest, and the strength that came with balance. It showed me that I could completely walk away from work and I would be fine. I didn't need to live a life chained to my career and work. I could live a life that included a personal and spiritual self. My friends cheered my progress and enlightenment. We laughed and toasted the gifts of friendship and love.

With everything cleaned up, I looked around as the last of the holiday energy swirled. I always loved how warm my home felt after the party was over. I could still feel the comfort of time shared with friends; the family I chose. As I looked around, I knew in my heart that this was quite possibly the last holiday I would have in this home. My eyes welled with tears as I recalled all the wonderful moments here. My castle, the safe haven I created for myself. It seemed time for me to move on. I didn't know where or when, and I was okay with only knowing at that moment that it was time.

I grabbed my last glass of wine and sunk into my bubble bath. I was certain 2011 was only the first glimpse at major change in my life. My physical stamina was the best it had ever been. I didn't know what was going to happen with the business, but I knew I would be okay regardless of the outcome. Emotionally, I was strong. I was living in a heightened state of awareness. I had come even deeper into my spirituality and my inner world; my soul was stronger, broader, and more capable. My ego was still out in front, but getting used to considering my heart's voice. I was stumbling less, and although I was still stuck on some things I was making great improvements. It was time for me to move on, leave the castle, and venture into the world. My heart was beating as strong as it ever had, and she was ready to run.

CHAPTER FIFTEEN

Finding Freedom

I started the year organizing the task of getting the house ready for market. After seven years, I had accumulated, and it was time to declutter. I was spending more time working on the exit and was picking up some momentum. I was running and training in the mild North Carolina winter and preparing for my next *personal* milestone – my first half marathon.

A Good Choice Made

The house went on the market in March, a week before the race. I trained diligently for months along with several friends also in quest of the same goal. It was an amazing moment when I crossed the finish line. The course was wet and my time was slower than my training pace, but I was overwhelmed at my capacity to achieve. I declared my physical self healed from the endometriosis the moment I hit that finish belt.

The house sold within three weeks and affirmed that I had made the correct choice. I had thirty days to move. I worked at a break neck pace to clear out, clean out, and reduce my "footprint." The day I moved into my home in 2004, it was 38 degrees and raining. The day I moved out, it was a sweltering 90 degrees. I had to keep the air conditioner off so as not risk blowing the compressor. It was more than 80 degrees inside; I was in a sweat lodge of my own making. The day was miserable and joyful all at the same time. I watched as my life was wrapped, packed, and loaded onto the truck where it would be transferred to storage vaults. The house had sold quickly; I hadn't made a definitive plan. I had an apartment scheduled to move into in six weeks, but had a strong sense I wouldn't end up there. I wasn't exactly sure when I would see my things again.

Later that night, I walked through the empty home as it was cooling off. In the darkness, I remembered all of the choices I had made in building it, what it looked like the moment I moved in, and now the moment I was leaving. I thought back to every party I hosted. I heard the laughter within these now empty rooms. I saw the lights in the corner where the Christmas tree once stood and remembered how each year that tree became something more beautiful than the year before because of my friends and the life I had made here. Laughter filled that home on many occasions, like the mornings my nieces were there and had jumped into my big mahogany sleigh bed, as we cuddled and planned our days. Upstairs the big room over the garage where I had my office. I wondered how much longer I would have the company and if I would I ever need an office like that again.

I thought of all the many tears too I considered all the healing that had taken place - physical, emotional, and spiritual. I stood in my kitchen and remembered all the meals, all of the moments I had nurtured myself and others there. My home was a part of me. It would always be a part of me and I would miss it; but it was time to move on to something new. I moved to Durham not knowing a soul and I realized how well I had created a life there. I hadn't the first clue where life would next take me, but I took courage in the task because of everything I lived, learned, and loved in that home, my castle.

In the kitchen, I left the new owner a fire extinguisher, a roll of paper towels, and a flashlight. The note read: "May you always be able to clean up any mess, put out any fire, and light your way through any dark moment. Welcome home." I included a small crystal heart of rose quartz with the note; a little part of my heart would always be in that home.

As I walked out my front door for the last time, I took one look and through my tears I said simply, "Thank you." Thank you for shielding me and harboring me. Thank you for showing me the love and compassion of people, and for showing me I have everything I need within me to be exactly who I'm to be. I pulled the door shut. The last things I picked up were the two red rocks placed on either side of the front door; that I had brought back from Cathedral Rock during one of my trips to Sedona. They grounded the home and connected it to my greater place in the world. It was time for them to find a new home, too.

At the closing, I met the young couple buying the house. They seemed excited and happy. They told me how much they loved it. They could tell how much I had loved it, and the great care I had given it was obvious. After my last signature hit the page, the attorney told me I could be on my way. I smiled, told them to enjoy their new home, and wished them a happy life there. I walked out with my good friend and realtor, gave her a big hug, and drove away. I realized in that moment that I didn't have the first clue where I was going or what would happen next. I considered how strangely calm I was with this feeling. I was not a person who operated without a plan, and while I had the makings of one, I had no clear destination in mind. I only knew of my next stop. The beach.

A Gypsy is Born

I picked up Sophie from the groomers and together we set out for a long weekend in Wilmington, North Carolina. I checked into a hotel and found something to eat. I went to sleep at 7:30 that night and slept more than twelve hours straight. If they say the sign of a good choice made is a good night's sleep, I would say I had made a great choice.

After three days of rest and quiet, I set off on the next phase of my adventure, a three-week travel extravaganza around the country. I had taken temporary shelter with my good friends across the street and their home became my checkpoint. Sophie and Finnegan were well provided for, and I was off to enjoy this sense of freedom. I called it "The Gypsy Tour" as I was at that moment, without a home and without a concrete perspective on my future. I was on my own, I was free, and I was at peace.

I landed in Sedona for my last week of the tour. I wondered what it would be like if I lived in Sedona for a while. Furnished home rentals were common and if I found a place, what about that? It might be a great experiment to see what Sedona would be like as a full time residence. It was my heaven, it was my haven, could it be my home? I quickly found a beautiful home at the base of Thunder Mountain. The owner allowed Sophie and Finnegan, and everything seemed to fall right into place.

Road Trip

I flew back to Durham, traded in my ten-year-old SUV for a Jeep, made arrangements for Finnegan to fly out, packed up Sophie and whatever else fit in the Jeep. On June 14, 2012, I set out on a cross-country road trip: Durham to Sedona. Sophie was my co-pilot and kept me company as we trekked the almost twenty-five hundred miles. I made three stops along the way, and each one offered me a little gift.

Nashville

Day One: Durham to Nashville. What a fun town. I loved the vibe in that city and we stayed at a hip and trendy hotel. I was a single woman, traveling alone with a small dog and a car packed with all my possessions. I decided to stay at places that would make me feel safe along the way. II felt comfortable there and put Nashville on the list of places to come and explore at some future point.

Oklahoma City

Day Two: Nashville to Oklahoma City. This was my longest day on the road, and it was also the most purposeful. Thirteen hours in the car and a lot of open road. Time to settle in on my thoughts. This day my mind wandered to a day seventeen years earlier, the day I found out that I wouldn't be able to have children, and that next morning, watching the horrific events of the Oklahoma City bombing. I spent most of the time in the car back on that couch, in that apartment, remembering everything I felt, and everything I watched. I remembered the chaos, the terror, the profound sadness and grief. I wondered what it would be like when I got there.

I walked from the hotel to the memorial and was awestruck. After living in Washington D.C., monuments and memorials were a familiar, almost transparent, part of the landscape. It was an obvious gesture of remembrance here. I walked up North Fourth Street and onto an overlook of the memorial. There are twin gates that frame the moment just before and just after the explosion, and serve as the entrances. The 9:01 gate marks the innocence of the city before the attack. The 9:03 gate represents that moment everything changed forever, and the hope that emerged from this absolute horror.[6]

I walked around the corner and saw a fence. The first one was installed to protect the site, and people immediately began to leave tokens. There have been more than sixty thousand items collected and the memorial includes a two hundred feet of fence that first framed this tragedy. This fence line continues to provide visitors opportunity to leave expressions of remembrance and hope.

I walked in through the 9:01 gate and stood at the reflecting pool. I was the only person there. I turned around and saw the chairs. The nineteen smaller ones represent the children that died that day. I marveled at the absolute sense of peace I found. It was almost dusk, the summer heat was still ablaze and the sky transitioning from bright blue to the most beautiful gray hue with bits of pink interspersed. I focused on the quiet, I looked up to the sky, and then I heard something. I looked around. I was the only one there, other than one security guard. I listened harder and heard it. Laughter. It was that high-pitched silly laughter of children playing. I looked into the chairs and saw them. They were sensations of energy, like big bubbles filled with sparklers. Children playing hide and seek on a warm summer evening. Waiting to catch the lightning bugs that were only moments away from casting their yellow glow, and offering a shining prize to their captor.

I felt a warmth spread through my entire body and deep into my soul. I looked and wondered if my children were there, the ones I was meant to have. I sensed deeply that they were, and the three that seemed to stand out from the others caught my attention. I took comfort that they were happy, playing with the others, waiting for the lightning bugs. I watched quietly, afraid to make a move. I didn't want to disturb them, I only wanted to hear the laughter. I reveled in the happiness I felt through them, because of them. I knew that I might never see them or feel them again, but to know that they were there and they were happy, somehow that seemed enough for the moment.

I stepped back and right onto the foot of the security guard. He asked me if I was okay, and I smiled through my tears and with the softest whisper I said "yes." He told me he was sorry that I couldn't have the dog at the memorial. I hadn't seen the sign. I apologized. He felt horrible, he hadn't wanted to disturb my private moment. It was quite rare to have the entire memorial to myself, a special moment indeed that he wished he didn't have to end for me. I smiled and told him it was okay. It was time for me to go anyway. I didn't want to be of any trouble, and was glad I had the opportunity to be there. I picked Sophie up and walked out through the 9:03 gate. I paused at the edge one last time. I said a quiet prayer for my children and asked that they be playful, joyful, and know that they would always be loved. I walked back to the hotel with the sounds of my children's laughter ringing in my ears, dancing straight into my heart.

Santa Fe

Day Three: Oklahoma City to Santa Fe. I faced the desolation of the southwest traveling from Oklahoma City to Santa Fe. The stretch of highway once I was west of Amarillo became desolate, and by the time I hit the New Mexico border, the sense of any life seemed distant if at all. This leg of the journey was probably the most bothersome to me. I was out in the middle of nowhere with no sense of life around me. It was hot, and at some point cell phone service became spotty and then ceased in some areas. When I arrived In Santa Fe, I was happy to see the beauty of the mountains and the movement of people and life. I enjoyed a delicious burrito and a couple of the coldest beers I think I have ever had.

During the night as I slept, the business experienced a significant issue. I awoke the next morning to discover several emails regarding a technology failure. I was able to speak with my partner briefly but he was in the throes of the nightmare. The one thing that was unclear was why he hadn't contacted me to discuss the problem and work together to formulate a plan. I read the email notification and in my mind I read through every performance clause, every non-performance clause, every back-up clause in our contracts. I had emails and phone calls from clients. I didn't have the first clue what to tell them because I wasn't certain myself what was happening.

Sedona

Day Four: Santa Fe to Sedona. As I packed up the car and set off for the final day of my journey, I couldn't help but see the prior day's drive as foreshadowing of this event. I was in the middle of nowhere with the sense that if I was stuck, it was possible I would have no resources available to help me. Here I was, looking at an email chain of disaster, in the middle of nowhere, with absolutely no ability to fix it.

As I drove west, I pondered the larger reason life had directed me to Sedona. As the barren desert of New Mexico gave way to the dusty desert of Arizona, the blank canvas allowed a clearer picture of purpose. It was time; the business was at its end. This was the ending of the business. I was being led to Sedona to navigate the final chapter. I negotiated major areas of construction that told me there was still a good amount of work to be completed, still challenges ahead of me. The horizon showed me light, and the light gave way to lushness as I drew nearer to Flagstaff. As I turned on to Highway 89-A and wound the car around the twisting descending roads into the Oak Creek canyon, I saw what would be the final twists and turns in this process. And then, the road started to open and straighten out and as I crossed Midgely Bridge, I saw Cathedral Rock in the distance. I knew that no matter what might happen along the way, I would be all right.

The Tree House

I settled into the house and picked up Finnegan from the airport. While he was not at all happy for his experience, he was happy to see me after our separation. My little family settled into that house at the base of Thunder Mountain. A huge juniper tree in front offered shade in the summer heat. It assured me of safety and security. Above all I knew that I was safe, I was protected, and I was loved. I felt that tree wasn't going to let anything pass that didn't belong. I placed the red rocks that had been at the door of my house in Durham at the front door of the house in Sedona. They had come full circle.

It wasn't quite two months before the business issue reached its crescendo. It included some difficult disagreements. The levels of anger and frustration were at moments surprising. My ability to stay in my heart, and keep my promise to be the quiet, gentle bear and not the angry grizzly was pressed to the limit. There were moments in the process where I thought that I would implode. I faced all sorts of "end state" scenarios in my mind. The first time I considered using the box of ugly. It was a true, real test of everything that I had learned. I needed desperately to pass the test.

After what became our final blow up, I felt we had three options. The business at the moment was going straight to zero. There was no way we could sustain our relationship and the business the way things were. We wanted two completely things with and for the company. We were competing with each other to make the other one see that we were each right; yet all we were doing was failing in the process. Our first option was to let the business go to zero. Take care of our clients and let contracts lapse, and not renew. Another option was to continue work to seek investors or acquisition. We had some traction with a couple of sources, but no guarantees that these would bear fruit. Our third option, was that one of us could buy the other out. I had a two-week business trip in front of me. We agreed to a cease-fire and would pick up our conversation when I returned. When we resumed our discussion, my partner told me he would like to make me an offer to buy my share. I lawyered up.

We launched into the negotiation phase of the deal and that brought more conflict. We seemed to both want the same end point, but we were kicking and screaming all the way to the door. My attorney assured me this was normal and in fact, we were actually doing better than some of the deals she had seen. Despite the tension and disagreement, she could sense there was a respect between us. We would get there.

Wisdom from an Old Friend

I connected with Scotty, a dear friend, confidante, and trusted advisor. He offered me great advice. He said it was simple, take the money, whatever money, and run. Don't walk, run. You have to trust that the universe will give you exactly what you need, to get you where you need to go.

Sometimes it gives you more, but it never seems to give you less. Trust the universe and get the deal done. Trust, there was that word again. I told him I loved him, sent him a hug, and an IOU for a big glass of wine and steak dinner next time I saw him. We realized we would both be in Chicago, but were missing each other by a couple of days. Next time.

I'll never forget this conversation with Scotty, as it was the last one he and I would have. He passed away during his trip to Chicago. He had issues with his heart and an aneurism, and was not in the greatest health, but he lived every day as if it was his last because he knew one day it would be. I diverted my plans, and redirected to Cleveland for the funeral. I hadn't been back to the town where I grew up for more than four years. Scotty was sending me there to say good-bye and to give me another more powerful lesson.

I drove past the bungalow that we lived in up until my dad died, and other spots that reminded me of my time growing up here. I went to Huntington Beach on Lake Erie every day. I sat at the edge of the pier on a rainy October morning and I heard Scotty. He was in that "limbo" space between this world and the next. He was laughing and happy. He was a little bewildered, his death had come quickly and he was a bit surprised. I told him it would settle for him soon, and told him to stay in the flow of things.

I heard him use a familiar tone, one that he would take on with me when I needed to pay attention. He said, "Nagel-T (his nickname for me), this is your home. No matter where you go in this world, you will always belong here and you can always return. Your home has nothing to do with the house you grew up in. You can be here, live here, and thrive here. Take your own advice, stay in flow of things, and go work that deal. It's all good."

In the middle of the night, I awoke with a start, and went immediately for pen and paper. I wrote down everything that came into my mind, the way it came to my mind. I wrote until my mind was absolutely empty. The next morning, I took those writings, and went to the coffee spot where Scotty and I used to meet when I was in town for a visit. I pulled out the writings and found my message, his message, and the message I needed. I consolidated those writings into a letter.

The letter was one I wrote to myself. In it, I acknowledged that I had run from the house where I grew up to find a life, a life I thought I was supposed to have. I ran away from the demons that haunted me. I stayed away, but was realizing now, that I could come back whenever I wanted, for as long as I wanted. I could do whatever I wanted while I was there. Then, in the rainy mess that Cleveland can be on a fall day, I went back to the beach. I took that letter and in the pouring rain, I set it on fire. And I stood back as I watched it burn completely, the ashes carried away in the rain and the wind. In that moment, I reclaimed my life, opened a space for whatever happened next, and I started to set myself free on a deeper level.

I thanked Scotty for all the gifts he had given me. This may have been one of his best. I would carry all of his sage advice in my mind, and his friendship in my heart. I toasted him with my mug of hot tea in the pouring rain and told him I was sorry we missed each other in Chicago. Next time.

Closing the Deal

Back in Sedona, my tree greeted me as I pulled into the drive, and it was time to get the deal done. Three brutal weeks later, my business partner flew out to Sedona, and we went through everything one last time. He sent instructions for the wire. We went out to lunch at a beautiful spot overlooking Schnebly Mountain and Snoopy Rock. My cell phone rang confirming the wire. The final papers were signed and that was that.

The next morning, he and I had coffee before he left. It was brief and mostly idle chatter. The substance of our working relationship had been negotiated through letters of intent, definitive agreements, and due diligence assessments. In the parking lot, I hugged him and wished him well, and he the same for me. After twelve years, I no longer owned the business I founded. We were divorced and I was free. I went back to the house and sat by the tree. I was a little bewildered. The tree seemed to lean in a bit to offer me a shoulder of sorts and I took its energy. After a long while, I went inside, and wondered what would happen next?

My lease in Sedona was up and I needed to get back to Durham, if only to figure out where I would go from there. I packed up, put Finnegan back on the plane, put Sophie and I on a plane, and headed back east. A good friend agreed to drive the car back on a quest for a cross-country experience. I was more than happy to oblige. I had no interest in driving. I wanted to fly.

New Years Check-in

I rented an apartment and had my stuff brought out of storage. It was nice to sit on my own couch and cook with my own things. I wasn't back more than a week or and I realized that this was only a temporary stop. I wasn't sure where I was going, but I knew that Durham was no longer my home.

What Durham was, and had always been, was my cocoon. The place where I could heal, learn, develop, and grow. I enveloped myself into this space and wondered what would happen when I was ready to break free. I had made a promise to myself, to the universe. If I was given the gift of release from this business, I would direct myself into the world in a manner that would help and serve others. I did not have the first clue how I would actually do that. But a promise was a promise after all and my first task was to figure out how to honor that promise.

On New Years Day, I hosted my feast and shared a meal with my friends. We laughed and shared stories, and a major catch up after my six-month sabbatical in Sedona. There was much to celebrate. I was happy for their company, as this New Year, there was cause for great celebration. I toasted a newfound peace, a sense of pure freedom, and a confidence in new direction and opportunity for the unlimited possibility life presents. I toasted the gifts of friendship, faith, forgiveness, and love.

After the last friend left, and the kitchen cleaned up, I again settled into a hot bubble bath with my last glass of wine. I marveled at my journey, and knowing that for all I had accomplished, I had only scratched the surface of what was yet to come. At that moment, I had no idea what would become of me, and I caught myself. Three years ago, I had been terrified and at the edge of an unknown. My ego had been running the show, putting together war plans in my head, preparing for an apocalypse. But my heart intervened and said no. And slowly but surely, my heart's voice had grown from a tiny whisper to a force to be reckoned with. Now I stood on a new edge, and wondered if I was ready for all that was about to happen. I believed it was possible to get to the other side of my survivor's instinct. I felt closer to my goal. I lifted my glass, took my last sip, heard the song in my heart, felt children's laughter deep in my soul, and was ready to dance.

CHAPTER SIXTEEN

Finding Purpose

I spent the next month doing what you might imagine... nothing. I trained for another half marathon if only to ensure that I got off the couch for a couple hours every day to exercise. I slept for hours at a time and caught up on television thanks to the technology of on-demand programming. I got tired of that quickly. It was soon time to figure out what was next.

Setting Some Structure

I had made a promise to live into my life's purpose. My problem was, I wasn't exactly sure what that meant. I had accumulated almost twenty-five years of professional experience and I had pretty substantive portfolio. It was important to me that whatever I created for myself filled me personally and professionally. It had to speak to my heart and my spirit. I wanted to engage with people and businesses on a personal level and help them find their path to whatever they chose.

It was like looking at an empty canvas, for as much as I had created and accomplished, in this moment, everything felt blank and new. I wanted to sketch in a vision, but I felt flustered. I had just lost the most significant layer of my identity. My business was no longer mine. I was grieving that loss and celebrating it at the same time. I was confused.

I was also concerned that there was a black spot that seemed to linger within me. I saw it every time I meditated. It was a catch I felt. I couldn't control when it showed up. It seemed to have a life all its own. I was confident that what was buried behind that black spot, that barrier were my remaining repressed memories. Ten years of therapy and four years of hard core "work" on changing patterns and behaviors and dropping the "survivor's instinct," there was still something left. What lived behind this barrier? I wondered when and if I would ever know.

In the meantime, I had to figure out what came next. I was about two weeks into my couch-sitting, television-watching respite, when I started contemplating this, and then, I met Eileen. She was a coach introduced to me by a good friend. Not even five minutes into our first conversation. I knew she would be the one to help me find my path. She wasn't going to draw it for me. She was going to challenge me to draw it for myself.

We went through some assessment work and landed on aspects of me that were rather unpleasant.

I could be inflexible and judgmental. I was emotionally distant in situations and was able to suspend emotions altogether when necessary. I used opinions to "escape" vulnerability. I was a fixer and a problem solver. If I had the smallest inkling something could go wrong, I got in there and fixed it. I needed to be believed. These were the core behaviors of that protective force inside of me. It wasn't my ego and it wasn't the adult persona. It was the unknown force field buried deeply inside me. For years, I had used the auspices of work as the rationale behind those behaviors. Work wasn't there anymore, and the behaviors remained.

An agenda was forming. I understood the scope of my work. From a practical training perspective, I wanted certifications in mediation and coaching. In April, I completed a certification program in mediation, and my first step into coaching certification began in June. The next thing on my plan was to take a trip and celebrate all I had accomplished. As my mind wandered to all the places I could go, it seemed to spin back to just one place. Hawaii.

Hawaii

I had a rare opportunity, and I had no real accountability to anyone or anything, with the exception of Sophie and Finnegan. I wanted a place that would take me as far away from life as I could get, for as long as I could manage. I was traveling alone. I wanted to be in a space where I only had to consider what I wanted to do and when I wanted to do something. Some place I had never been, a place where I could be true to what I was, *free.*

On the flight out, I sat next to a lovely older man named David, it struck me because that was my dad's name. Any time I meet a David, I always look to see if a little of my dad was looking back at me. I definitely saw him in this David. It was an eight-hour flight and we had time to chat. He asked me about my dad, and how he felt at the prospect of his daughter taking off on her own. I told him my dad had died when I was a little girl. I shared that he would be a little nervous. However, there was not a lot he would have been able to do to change my stubborn mind. He and I were the same that way. He would worry and delight in the adventure. He would make me call him every day to tell him I was okay, that I loved him, and give him the chance to tell me the same. I was his sunshine.

David went into Dad mode. He told me I should go to the Big Island and take a helicopter tour to see Mt. Kilauea. It is rare to see an active volcano, and I shouldn't miss it. The concierge would take care of it and I should let them. Go to the Halekulani Hotel and have drinks and an early dinner at the House Without a Key. Make sure I have a room that faces the park, that way I would be able to see the fireworks. Try to stay awake until sunset. It will go a long way to fighting the jet lag. The first couple of days would be tough, but I would settle in, and it would be just fine if I wanted dinner at 3 pm.

He gave me his cell phone number. He had business and was completely booked. If his plans changed, he would love to treat me to dinner and celebrate my accomplishment. He gave me the cell phone number of the general manager at one of the hotel properties where he was a part owner. I was to call him if I needed anything at all. He would know to pick up the call and take care of it. He said I needed to be comfortable that I had help if I needed it. I smiled because I wasn't sure whether I needed to be comfortable, or David did. Either way, I was touched deeply by the gesture.

As we landed, David leaned over to me and told me that he thought I was a beautiful woman, smart and capable, deserving of this celebration, and everything wonderful that life has to offer. He was quite certain that my father was extremely proud of the woman I had become and happy to know I was living my life as completely as I was. He also felt that no matter what path I chose, I would be brilliant, and I should keep taking risks. I thanked him and did my best to keep from crying but my eyes welled anyway. As we deplaned, he said, "You have a good time, Sunshine." I don't know if I misheard or if he actually called me Sunshine. It caught my throat. Then I heard him talking on the phone about me. I smiled and said a quiet "Thanks, Daddy."

I was greeted with my first lei, beautiful white shells and dark kukui nuts when I arrived in Waikiki. I was on the twenty-second floor and opened the door to my first lanai, a beautiful view overlooking the park. I didn't even have to ask, they already picked a room for me, and confirmed I had a beautiful view of the fireworks on Friday night. I unpacked, showered, and ordered room service. I enjoyed dinner *and* sunset on the lanai.

Just Enjoy the Splash

I addressed the tourist aspects of my trip on Oahu. I spent an amazing day at Pearl Harbor and Punchbowl Cemetery. I made arrangements with the concierge and flew to the Big Island for the helicopter tour into the volcano. I ran Diamond Head a couple of times and had an early dinner at the House Without a Key. I shopped a local farmers' market, walked along the beach, and sat in the park and read. I watched the sunset every night on the lanai.

I took a paddleboard lesson courtesy of the surf shop up the street. The owner shared with me the most important lesson regarding the board. Stay balanced and focused. If you fall, just fall. Don't drop to your knees and don't try to grab the board. Just fall and enjoy the splash. We made a deal that he would never disclose how many times I fell that day. A couple of sea turtles joined me on this maiden voyage and showed me how to work the strong currents of Waikiki.

Mother's Day (figures)

I decided to take a driving adventure around the island on my last full day on Oahu. I wanted to take a couple of short hikes and check out the North Shore. The concierge helped me map my entire journey, including options to stop for lunch or a drink along the way. It was Mother's Day, but they were confident they could sneak me in most anywhere I wanted.

Mother's Day. Shit. I had forgotten this day was upon me. It had been three years since I had spoken with my mother. Every Mother's Day for the past three years, I did something special to honor her. One year, I cooked her favorite foods. Another year I planted some flowers. This year, it appeared I was going to honor her on Oahu. I was going to drive around the island, hike and see the beauty that is the North Shore.

I set out, at dawn, to the first stop, the Koko Crater Railway Trail. From here I would travel to Makapuu Point Lighthouse, also on the eastern shore. After that it was off to the North Shore and lunch somewhere. It would be a drive, but I was looking forward to seeing the island. The hotel packed a couple of beach bags, including one with some water and snacks for me. With the top down, I was all set.

Waikiki was beautiful. The sun was just rising and there was not a cloud in the sky. As I made my way east, I noticed the sky turned gray and clouded, and then a light mist began to fall. I had to pull over to put the top up, as I was driving straight into a tropical downburst. As I got closer to where I was supposed to turn for the Koko Crater hike, I noticed the traffic lanes were blocked. A half-marathon was in progress and the traffic was being diverted. I drove in circles trying to get where I needed to be. I looked up at the top of the crater and it was completely socked in by a thundercloud. There would be no hike. I wound myself out of that mess, around the race and found a Starbucks. I asked the person behind me if he knew about the weather on the North Shore. He told me it wasn't going to be any better over there, as that part of the island was socked in with rain, as well. The rain wouldn't give way any time soon and Waikiki was the best place to be, and his best advice was to head that way. My trip was scrapped, and I wouldn't have a chance to reschedule as I was leaving in the morning. It was Mother's Day. Figures.

Maui

On my last morning, Oahu greeted me with a beautiful rainbow. To believe, to listen, and to trust were the messages I received as I packed the last of my things and set off for Maui. The minute I stepped off the plane in Kahului, I went into total relaxation mode. The air smelled like flowers and the sky was beautiful. A gentle breeze was calling to me. I put the top down, plugged my phone into the audio system, hit shuffle and let the music play.

The resort in Wailea greeted me with a lei of fresh flowers. The bellman opened the door to my room and brought in my things. Waiting there for me was a beautiful bottle of wine and a pineapple cake. I was in heaven. The card was from a good friend saying, "Congratulations, enjoy your celebration and reward, you earned this." The bellman opened the wine, poured me a glass and sat me on the lanai. I looked out over the ocean and the light clouds in the sky. "Congratulations Ms. Nagel, I understand you are here to celebrate the sale of your company and wish you a relaxing visit with us. We are here to make sure you have just that." He handed me a "kitchen stock" list of items that I might want to order for the room. He would be happy to take care of it for me right away and that I would not be disturbed once these "administrative" tasks were completed. Oh, and would I like to have a reservation for dinner or prefer room service? He could help with that as well. He suggested I take a moment and enjoy my wine and he'd be right back.

I thought of the last time I had been seated on a lanai, except it was a balcony in Sedona, four years earlier. It was cold and night, and the bellman was just as kind as he handed me a glass of wine. I had been beyond exhausted and finished with my life. I wasn't even sure I wanted to live. I was lonely, hurt, confused, and unsure.

On that day, I looked out over the lanai and into the ocean, the waves cresting, and the clouds shifting in the sky. I saw a heart emerge in the clouds. I couldn't believe that for everything I felt that night in Sedona, I felt absolutely the opposite on this afternoon. The sun, the light, the happy, the purpose coming into focus. I was alone, but not lonely. I was just starting to come out of that cocoon and into the world. I was letting others help me take care of me.

The bellman returned. He stocked the pantry and made arrangements for my dinner on the lanai. As I started to get up, he waved me away, and said, "Don't worry, you relax, I'll be around if you need anything else." I thanked him. I made sure this time I had his name and the number where I could reach him. I remembered that night in Sedona when he told me not to worry, and then I couldn't find him the next morning.

I slept the soundest sleeps in Maui, with the doors open and the sound of the ocean waves lulling me to dreamland. I walked every morning on the beach and felt the softest sand scrunch between my toes. I walked into the waves and felt the pull of the ocean. The unbelievable service continued as I found my spot on the beach and table for breakfast. The sweetest woman remembered me every morning and I didn't have to ask for the fresh pineapple after the first day. It arrived with my iced tea. She asked me every morning if I was having pancakes, again. It's my secret with her how many mornings I had pancakes.

In advance of my trip, a mutual friend introduced me to Pono, a private tour guide. She assured me he was the best person to help me explore Maui and she was absolutely correct. I wanted to connect deeply into Maui's spiritual essences and special energies, and understand why I had been drawn there. Pono greeted me with a fresh lei of plumeria from his own garden, and I wore it all day, allowing the amazing scent to draw into me. He plotted out a day visiting spiritual ruins and healing areas of the island. He was thoughtfully respectful of the land and my connection to it. I was able to spend as much time as I wanted at each spot. I made offerings, meditated, and prayed at several sacred sites.

I brought the crystals I used with my chakra and meditation work with me. I washed these in the fresh waterfalls near the Waihe'e Ridge, and set some intentions for my future. I then left five crystals in the grooves of a lava stone near the waters edge. I left two pieces of citrine for abundance, luck, and love, and one piece of moonstone for serenity, compassion, and intuition. I added one piece of blue topaz, known as the writer's stone. It helps generate strength and creativity in the written and spoken word. The final crystal was sugilite, representing protection, forgiveness and spirituality. Sugilite is also about love as it helps open the heart chakra to unconditional love.[7] After I enjoyed the sweetest, freshest fruits like sun-ripened pineapple and strawberries. My strong bond with Maui began that day and I felt it a home I never knew and was glad to have found. I slept that night with the wilting plumeria on my pillow.

Haleakala

The capstone event on that island took place on May 18, 2013. I was going to watch the sunrise at Haleakala Crater. Pono agreed to take me to a local spot. It wasn't a tour. It was two new friends sharing one of the most beautifully spectacular events in the world.

The phone rang at 2:20 am. "Good morning Ms. Nagel, this is your wake up call. Would you like us to call back in ten minutes?" I mumbled, "No, thank you." I hung up, blinked a couple of times and had a good stretch. I flipped off the covers, grateful that I set out my clothes and organized my pack before going to bed.

Getting ready, I paused and looked in the mirror. I thought of every time I had looked into the mirror and forced myself to see the real me. I had thrown many rocks at those mirrors, shattering the toxic patterns that had lived within me. I knew that I still had a few rocks to throw. Something still eluded me. The black spot. However, as I stood in front of my mirror on that morning, I was happy with what was looking back at me.

I was out the door in twenty minutes, still half asleep but right on schedule. The car was waiting in the front and the bellman said, "Good morning, Ms. Nagel we have your car ready. I put the top down, packed in some blankets, a couple of pillows, towels, and here." He handed me a go-mug of hot tea. I smiled gratefully and asked him how many times he had been He responded, "Only a couple, but it's beautiful. Enjoy!"

With that he shut me into the car and I pulled out of the drive. I drank in the essence of plumeria. This morning was the moment I had no idea I had been waiting for, and it was finally here. I met Pono, and we packed in his stuff. He took the keys, tucked me into the passenger's seat with a pillow and blanket, and told me to take a nap. It would be almost two hours until we arrived.

I fell fast asleep and awoke about an hour later. I looked up into the night sky and saw what I'm sure were a million stars. I saw them each distinctly and collectively as they lit the sky. I thought of the night at the ballpark in Chicago and on the balcony in Sedona. There had been many moments that I had looked into the sky to find my life and saw nothing but black. Not this morning. The heavens shone brightly, to be certain that I saw every speck of light I had never seen.

We arrived at Haleakala National Park. The temperature dropped as we wound our way to the top, and I was grateful for the heated car seats. I was wide awake as we closed in on our destination. In the end, that last hike was quite short compared to the many I had taken over the past four years. We rounded the corner and I saw the volcanic crater for the first time. It took my breath away, my heart pounded. I had a sharply distinct experience from the one on the Big Island. There, I saw steam, fire, and the destruction that the lava path had cut through the land it torched. It had its own beauty, mostly tinged in grays and blacks as the lava marbled and settled into the mountainside.

Here I saw brilliant shades of orange, red, brown, and green. It was peaceful and the beauty was indescribable. Vibrant life and color exploded in front of me as I experienced what happens after the fire. The life that sprung forth from the black and gray was breathtakingly beautiful. I was sitting on top of the world, the sky above and the clouds below, and the spectacular craters to my right. The entire vista was mine. A quiet final end and a calm beginning, I looked down and found a heart shaped rock at my feet and I knew I had arrived.

I remembered all of the hearts I had found along the way, in the rocks, on the trails, in the sky, the trees. It seemed they were everywhere. Each one inspired me to continue along and stay committed to the ultimate goal – finding my heart and finding love. My heart had been quite weak in the beginning, and now it beat boldly and strong. It too, was ready.

Pono poured me some tea and I bundled up. It was thirty-eight degrees. Pono offered me a gift. It was a lei of rare white kukui nuts that he had made for me. In ancient Hawaii, kukui oil was used to make light. The nut offered light, hope, renewal, and protection. The nuts carry your own Mana or spiritual energy. It lasted forever and could carry energy from one generation into the next.

I connected my Bluetooth® speaker and hit play. A meditation mantra I had been given a few years earlier began to fill the quiet with a peaceful rhythm. I was told the Dalai Lama offered this particular mantra as he was helping a friend make his final transition from this life to the next. The transition was not a journey of loss or trauma, but a joyful journey at the correct time, with the understanding of life beyond earth. As we listened, Pono offered a Hawaiian prayer to welcome the sun. I was literally living that mantra, letting one life give way to another; leaving the darkness and welcoming the light.

In the final moments of night, as the sky transitioned from black to a beautiful purplish gray and the stars started to dim, I thought of my children and was at peace knowing they were still playing. My mind then went to my three beautiful nieces I had carried with me along my journey. While every choice was mine, they were the whisper in my ear, knowing every choice was as much about them as it was about me.

I held my breath as I watched the sun work through the clouds and bear light and truth to the new day. My end and my beginning were one for a moment, and then the sun peeked above the clouds. The first moment of my new beginning. I stared straight into the light, I let it envelope and warm me. I felt my heart pounding and then I heard a child's laugh. It was small and quiet, almost a giggle, like they couldn't believe what they were seeing. It was the little girl, the seven-year-old, my heart. She represented all of the kind, good and loving things I wanted for myself and others. I smiled as I saw her step away from the castle, into the light. She looked at me, and I nodded and told her quietly, "Yes. It's okay. You can go and play now. Everything is okay. We are okay." I saw her skip across the rocks and right onto a cloud and she just laughed all the way.

After that it was still except for a very soft, gentle wind that appeared here and there. It was beautiful. I couldn't take my eyes off the sun, and I drank in the warmth and strength of the light. I saw myself in this moment. Writing at a small desk on my laptop with a mug of tea and soft music playing in the background. Speaking in front of large groups. Sitting quietly with someone who was somehow hurt, and I was present to help heal them. Walking on paths and talking with people endlessly. There were thousands of hugs for adults and children.

My story. Tell my story, was what I heard. I then heard the voice ask me if I would live into my destiny, my soul's true purpose in this life, and I nodded and said a quiet, yes. I promise. I will.

I'm not sure how long we sat there, and then Pono spoke. "Who are you? How did you do this?" He had tears in his eyes. He said, "I have lived on this island thirty years and watched the sunrise here hundreds of times, and I have never seen anything as beautifully amazing as this. Who do you know up there to put on this kind of a show? Who are you?"

I smiled and shrugged. "I guess we're about to find out, aren't we?"

CHAPTER SEVENTEEN

Finding a Speck of Light

I returned from Hawaii relaxed, hopeful, and excited. A few weeks later, I was on a plane bound for Santa Barbara to attend a four-day seminar called LifeLaunch™ at the Hudson Institute of Coaching. It's an intensive, self-discovery retreat and the first step of their coaching curriculum. I felt well-practiced in the art of self-discovery by this point, and was curious to see what else there was to learn.

Be careful what you wish for.

The Black Spot Cracks

It was a bumpy plane ride from Durham to Los Angeles, and I settled in with music and some light meditation. It was clear and I looked out the window far into the horizon. My mind started to drift to that one black spot. I asked my mind, my spirit, my whole being to shine some light into this dark corner. I needed to clean out this gunk. Whatever was on the other side of that spot was the final piece of my life's puzzle. I found myself crying. Not heaving sobs, but rather, a steady almost silent cry where tears were streaming down my face. I couldn't make the tears stop. I was a little girl, it was after my father died. It was at the townhouse. I had no memory of any moment in that townhouse. I couldn't see anything, but felt tremendous fear. I heard a voice telling me to hide. That was it, but it was enough. It was the first flash of another memory.

A Reunion

On my way to LifeLaunch™, I stopped in Simi Valley to visit Lisa, one of my best friends from high school. After five minutes, it was as if only a day had passed since we last saw each other. We talked for hours and hours. I shared my issues regarding my repressed memories and what I had experienced on the flight out. She shared with me as much as she remembered about our growing up. I trusted her immediately and completely, and was grateful that life had twisted us back around to find each other. There's something about the connection with and comfort of a childhood friend. Lisa gave me a sense of support and encouragement and a context to my past. She was there to help me any way she could.

A Big Boulder on the Beach

LifeLaunch™ helped me begin to place the spiritual and emotional aspects of my journey into a structured, intellectual context. It showed me how I may be able to put my experience into practice for others. I started to understand the reprogramming and unlearning of that which remained, the protector within.

There is a part of the retreat called Bouldering. It's where you acknowledge the obstacle that keeps you from reaching goals. These blockages commonly take root in the form of inner voices we create in ourselves, or ones that are given to us, often during our childhood. I was coming to understand exactly why I had been led there, and what I was supposed to do with my "boulder," the black spot. I was unable to trust and had a fear of intimacy and vulnerability, and realized whatever existed behind the spot was the source. Guarding, judgment, and inflexibility were my remaining go-to response and defense mechanisms. These were the construct of the protector within me. While I was not yet certain of all that had taken root during those years at the townhouse, whatever happened to me began there. I didn't yet know the details, but what happened there taught me how to be this way.

No surprise, I was afraid. I called Eileen for her perspective. She had participated in the same program with Hudson. I told her what had transpired and the picture that was forming. Dots were starting to connect. I knew I needed to push this "boulder" in the hope that it would help open a space, and encourage my memory to keep moving. I knew I had to be patient, but this was an important nudge of encouragement. I was afraid to trust, and yet it was precisely what I needed to do. Eileen assured me that I was in a safe space. Trust myself first by following my instinct, she said, and stay in awareness of my feelings. Then lean into trusting others as best I could.

On the beach before we started, I kicked up a stone in the sand. It was in the shape of a heart. I picked it up and held it in my hand. I told my new friends how I found hearts everywhere. Outside the circle on the beach was a band of ravens. The ravens came to me in the early days of my journey and I found them an enlightening totem. They are highly intelligent and represent the power of thought and active search for information. They represent the ability of the mind to intuit meaning and allow it rather than hunt for it. The raven asks you to believe in magic and trust it to bring joy, understanding, and fulfillment. There were about ten of them on the beach as I began my work, and I found this fitting and comforting.[8]

I stood on the beach and told these eight people that I had known not even two days before about what I had experienced. In the last few days, a tiny light started to shine through a pinhole crack on the black spot. I knew this was a beginning and I had no idea how or when it would finish. These inner voices that lived within me, and told me I was trouble. I was a problem, and I was lying. I wasn't worth it. Don't tell, "they" won't believe you anyway. These eight people supported me in my work, they allowed me to be vulnerable, and they helped me heal. I leaned into people I barely knew, and I trusted them. It was beautiful to watch them support me, without condition. I was enriched, enlivened, and elevated. I believed that if I could trust them, it was possible for that pinhole of light to explode at some point.

The Way of the Bear

I returned from California and prepared for my next stop. My niece was getting married and asked me to come to Cleveland for the wedding. As I agreed to it, I also agreed to be in the company of my mother, whom I had not spoken with in more than three years, and my brother whom I had not spoken with in more than seven years. It was time to consider a new possibility with my family. I struggled greatly with how I would "show up" during this event. Part of me wanted to slip in the back of the church, watch the ceremony, and leave. My niece wanted me there for the entire event and I considered how I might accommodate this request given the strife, distance and estrangement within this family system. I contemplated what lesson life was getting ready to teach me. I was living the way of the bear. The question was, which aspect of the bear wanted to appear. The peaceful, tranquil soul that wandered the earth, or the fierce protector ready to defend myself at all costs. I decided to lean into to the former and not the latter.

I grabbed two pieces of jade that I had carried for years, and two heart rocks from Sedona and set off for Cleveland. Jade carries many healing properties and promotes balance, wisdom and peace; it repels negative energy and encourages stability.[9] I was quite conflicted with respect to the relationship I had with my mother, and the pieces of my life that still didn't connect. I felt no maternal relationship with her, yet she was my mother. The child within me wanted desperately for her to open up, clear any darkness, and choose me. The little girl wanted her to see the heart, my heart, and wanted to feel as if it was the most important thing to her. The adult was able to see her as a person, flawed and imperfect, and possibly incapable of doing any of these things. I did my best to stay open, but history was not on my side here, and I was managing expectations.

I wrote a letter to my mother in an effort to create a space, and an opening for my family. I gave it to her a few days before the wedding. In the letter, I acknowledged the experiences of my father's death and its impact on our lives. I sought out Buddha and in the letter quoted, "Pain is inevitable, suffering is choice." Pain is something that comes to us. It's a part of life. Suffering is what we do to ourselves. Grief falls somewhere between pain and suffering. Grief provides the opportunity to release pain and find life's lesson. I hoped her life was free of suffering. I gave her one piece of the jade and one of the heart rocks from Sedona.

It seemed to me that she received the letter well, yet the question in my head remained, was she ready and capable of meeting me in this space? Time would tell. The next morning, I visited a place I hadn't been in decades, the cemetery where my father and uncle are buried. I weeded both plots and burned some sage along with some of my dad's pipe tobacco. I sat there for a while and talked to them both. I told them how much I missed them. I loved them and lived in honor of them each day of my life. I then took the second heart rock from Sedona and dug a small pit on the backside of my father's grave marker. In the pit, I placed the second piece of jade, and I packed the heart tight around it into the ground. A gentle wind swept through the cemetery. I leaned into it and felt the gentle comfort of my dad's hug. I released the story between my mother and father. Whatever transpired between them was between them once again.

Driving back to the hotel, I recalled what Scotty said to me on the pier that day. I could always be there, my hometown. I would always be welcome. It occurred to me that it would be a great place to write my book, spend time with my nieces, and complete my coaching certification. It might help with my memory. Three days later, I rented a home not far from the one where I grew up. I was moving to the last place I ever expected, Cleveland.

Happy Holidays?

I hosted my family for all three holidays – Thanksgiving, Christmas and New Year's Day. It was exhausting, but I wanted to make an investment in family. I had visited for the holidays in the past, but I lived there now. I wanted to experience the family dynamic from my new perspective on life. I knew a lot, but also knew there were still some things hiding from my conscious awareness.

We gathered on Thanksgiving. Having spent many holidays with my friends, I was used to long days spent talking, watching football, and lots of wine and laughs. Those were casual, lingering, low-stress kind of days. On that Thanksgiving, I learned about an unspoken rule within my family, the four-hour rule. It seemed four hours was the maximum amount of time my family could be in the same place. I didn't sense there was leeway, it was a hard stop. Dinner was a little late to the table and everyone seemed antsy to me and I watched eight people plow through their dinner and rush through the kitchen to help me clean and pack leftovers. As I pulled out the homemade pies, I noticed everyone was getting ready to leave. They all agreed to take some... to go. Time had expired on this event.

For Christmas, I was ready. I moved through the meal, we opened gifts, and everyone left. Four hours almost on the dot. On New Year's Eve, I prepared for my feast and I spent a quiet evening alone watching a random slide show of all my adventures from the past year. This New Year's Day was the first in many years I would not be joined at the table with my closest friends. I missed them greatly. I started this New Year with my family. There didn't seem to be much excitement over my southern fare. After everyone left, my youngest niece and I went out for a while. I wanted to start this New Year breaking a little from tradition and looking out into the world to see if there was something new in the offing.

Back home, I poured my last glass of holiday wine, and soaked in the small bathtub of my rental home. I enjoyed the vanilla and sandalwood bubbles. I considered all I had accomplished. I was definitely on a new path and curious what was around the corner. It felt weird being here. My memory had been silent since the bouldering on the beach in Santa Barbara. I knew being here was the best chance I had to break open this memory. I was somehow making progress. As I took my last sip of wine, I toasted to a new year full of promise and wished for that deep happiness that comes with resolve.

CHAPTER EIGHTEEN

Finding Truth

My first Cleveland winter in twenty years also went on record as one of the worst in the city's history. It was cold, seriously cold. I learned a new weather term - the polar vortex. I tried to look on the bright side, these weather patterns were leaving me indoors for days at a time and providing a perfect opportunity to write. I distanced myself from my family using the cold weather and writing demands as the reason for the space. I craved time to be alone with my thoughts and mind.

I spent long days and nights at my desk, juggling school and writing. Part of my school curriculum required me to work with another coach, and in this came an amazing gift, Lynn. She and I worked well together from the minute we spoke. She had a powerful, gentle manner in asking questions and drawing out my perspective. She became my first "publisher." I created a timeline for my writing and tied deliverables to our coaching sessions. This gave me a sense of structure and process.

I started writing in a more traditional form, from an outline, and then building content from that outline. I then worked iteratively to add detail. I found early on that my best writing time was evening. It's dark and there are fewer distractions. I was a little tired from the day and it seemed easier to tap into my subconscious. I started around six or seven in the evening and wrote until two or three in the morning. It was when I started working on the "fill in" portions, that my memory began responding. I encouraged my subconscious mind to stay open and allowed creative energy to flow. I was slowly chipping away at the resistance, the protector.

In the moments when I was in an open space, words appeared on the page. Clues, memories, things I felt and smelled and tasted. When I landed on something unfamiliar I resisted at first, and caught myself trying to correct what I was writing. It was then that I realized there was no need to correct, I was writing a truth. It was coming from a small quiet voice deep inside my soul. It was the protector and I encouraged it to keep going. I asked every day to remember something, it was okay, I was ready. Lisa helped me greatly during this time. I read her pages, and she asked me questions regarding what she heard within my writings. She provided context to our childhood, and helped me find clues in my words. She caught things I didn't, and we explored them together. She was open, honest, helpful, trusting, and loving toward me.

A Vulture's Blessing

It was late March, past my birthday, and I was making great progress on my writing. Bits and pieces of my memory had come back. They weren't great memories. Anger, rage, fear were the overtones of many. I remembered being dragged, pulled, and shaken. I felt nauseous and dizzy and like my motion was always slow or somehow hindered. I wanted to run, but it was as if there was a big belt around me preventing me from getting where I needed to go. I smelled sweat and other odors like mothballs. I asked my mind to keep going. Whatever voice was speaking, it needed to keep talking.

I hit a bit of a fumble with my writing; I stalled some with my progress, and thought it reasonable given that I had been writing non-stop for several weeks. It didn't feel like a block, more like fatigue. I needed a break. I felt a bit more agitated and that was an uncommon sensation for me. I had a dull headache. The kind that won't stop you, but it won't let you go either. I couldn't shake it. On March 24th, I decided to take the day off and catch up on some errands.

I ran into my stepfather during one of my stops. I asked him if he was behaving himself. He came up to me in a strange way that felt eerily familiar. I thought I smelled alcohol and was struck by the way I reacted to the way he was looking at me. Chills went up my spine and bile kicked up into my throat.

I was shaken as I drove home and decided to stop at Huntington Beach and clear my head. It was cold, but the beach was a comfort zone for me. I walked the path to the stairways leading down to the sand and water and that's when I saw them. Turkey vultures.[10] I lost count after twenty. They were flying low and as I made my way down the stairs, they swooped in and around me. I had never experienced anything like it before. I felt they were pulling something from me. I stopped midway in my descent on the stairs and watched them.

Turkey vultures may not be the most beautiful creature from a physical perspective but their purpose is. They are a powerful spirit animal and common Native American totem. They are cleaners. They will eat something rotten and then excrete something clean and non-toxic. They seek out and process rot, and leave something clean behind. It's not the first time the turkey vulture has come to me, and despite the magnitude of their presence, I wasn't afraid of them. When they do appear, I consider three aspects. First, how many appear. The most I had seen was five or six on one or two occasions. I usually saw two or three at most and often just one. Today, there were almost *thirty* and maybe more.

Second, I note how close the vultures are in relation to the ground. When they are high aloft in the sky, I think of them as skimming off the top layers, just tidying up on things like a feather duster. The closer they are to the ground, the bigger the mess. If they are on the ground, it's significant. There were at least a dozen on the ground. Third, I discern the vulture's relationship to me. The more engaged they are with me, the more it's about me. There were several within arm's length of me. As I approached the beach, some of the grounded vultures took flight and hovered and flew low around me in a circular motion. Almost like scrubbing a spot. They swooped up, around and down in a slow, graceful circular motion, like a carefully, beautifully choreographed dance. They danced around me in flight and were close enough could reach out and touch them. Each one was there for me, to clean out the gunk.

I heard Scotty's voice tell me it was okay, go home, it would be fine. I heard my dad tell me he loved me; go home; it would be fine. I was not afraid; I was awestruck by the beauty of their movement, and the blessing they carried. I knew something big and messy was about to happen, but I knew I was safe and protected. The vultures were there to help me clean a mess. I turned around and ran up the steps. The vultures continued their movement until I made it to the car. I went straight home.

Chill Out... Have a Beer

I unpacked groceries and considered what was happening. I tended to some chores around the house. I called Lisa to tell her and was surprised what I found on the other end of the phone. Lisa was in bed and she had been in bed all day. She had a splitting headache, she couldn't move. She had been crying and was overwhelmed with a sense of grief. She had no idea where this came from, and she couldn't seem to control it. This was *highly* unusual behavior for Lisa, as she rarely fell incapacitated. I told her what happened to me. She was agitated, confused and unsure as well. It was like we were mirrors, except she was in a space of grief and sadness and I was in a space of unknown. I couldn't process or function, couldn't get any work done, and was in no mood to write. She told me to rest, take the rest of the day, and cook something comforting for dinner. Chill out and have a beer.

I took her advice, opened a beer, and made dinner. After, I picked away at some chores. I switched up my music to try and break the mood. My headache intensified and I became more agitated. I was restless. I had another beer. I was circling through this process and I was walking in circles in my house. I was cleaning, scrubbing, organizing. I kept walking around in circles trying to figure out what was happening, and then it hit me.

The Black Spot Explodes

I was in the process of recovering another memory. There was quite a bit of fight with it, yet I wouldn't relent. I kept repeating, 'it's okay, I'm ready, let go.' Please let this happen. I went to my office and pulled a chair in front of the mirror and centered myself. The tears began to fall almost immediately. The same tears from the plane ride out to Santa Barbara. I smelled it first. Alcohol, the stench combined with stale cigarettes was breathed upon me and somehow it felt like a poison seeping out of my skin. The sweat came next and it was slimy and putrid. I was overcome with nausea and dizziness, like I was awakening from a drug-like or drunken stupor. I kept staring in the mirror as the room spun around me. Stay centered, stay in reality, and let go. *Please* let go.

The physical pain came next. It was sharp and intense. It was unlike any other pain I had felt before. Something was being forced into my body over and over again. The pain was excruciating as I felt the force tear through my body. I was trying to pull away from myself and I couldn't. I was fighting it. My neck squelched and my hands felt tied. I had sensations of being dragged and pinned.

Next came sound. I heard voices. Male voices. They were familiar but I wasn't clear. There was laughter, evil laughter. There were warnings. Stay still, I'm not finished with you. The last thing to clear was the vision. The faces were eerily similar. The eyes were wild, bloodshot, and piercing. The laughter was booming and evil. The words whispering in my ear were disgusting. I saw myself quietly screaming to make it all stop, to make it go away, to please let me die and let it end. Please let me go to heaven to be with Daddy.

I kept looking in the mirror, and told myself this was memory. It wasn't happening at this moment, I was remembering what happened. I was not living in it again. I was safe. Then my entire body crumpled and I melted out of the chair and onto the floor. The tears turned into heaving sobs and then came the screaming. I screamed for every moment I wasn't able to as a child. I was writhing in pain and overwhelmed by what I was remembering. The voices, the smells, the visions. The pain, it was immense and it wouldn't stop.

I have no idea how long I was on the floor or how loud I screamed. There were moments I was convulsing for air. I crawled to the phone, plugged in 911, and set the phone on the floor beside me. I didn't want to call. If they came, they would sedate me, and I might forget. As horrific as this was, I didn't want to forget. I was finally remembering. The black spot was exploding and showing me what it had masked. I felt it ripping from the dark of my memory. I felt it tearing away from my soul.

I laid on the floor and a wave of calm came over me. I centered myself as best possible and focused on my breathing. I stared at the phone, and wondered. Who did I tell? I asked again and again. Who knew? And then it came through, almost as if it was the last breath of life from this spot. The final explosion. It was my mother's voice. I heard yelling, yet I couldn't make out the words. I felt fear and anger directed toward me. I heard the door slam with me on the other side, alone. I was a child alone.

I spiraled into another cycle of intense, cataclysmic emotion. I was overwhelmed with the realization that this happened to me. It was before they were married.

After awhile, I'm not sure how long, it grew quiet again. I heard another quiet voice, almost as a whisper. It was Scotty. His tone was consistent and steady and the message kept repeating. "You have a standing invitation on the North Shore." North Shore? My mind went immediately to the North Shore in Oahu. The one place I hadn't been able to get to on my trip. Hawaii. Oahu. Maui and Haleakala. I thought about my sunrise and kept hearing his calming repetitive voice. I tried to picture it in my mind and I started to calm down. I didn't understand except to know something existed on the other side of all of this and I was welcome. I heard the sound of waves crashing on the shore.

I felt my dad's presence as I came out of this final cycle. He was angry and grief-stricken. He heard me when I told him that no matter what he felt at that moment, from wherever he was, at this moment there was only one person that mattered, me. I couldn't support anything or anyone other than me. I thought of the turkey vultures and what they had been sent to do. They were given to me to help me clean up this horrific nightmare that had lived within me all of these years. They were going to help me clean up this mess, to replace the rot with something clean.

When things seemed to plateau and I thought I could actually speak to someone, I texted Lisa. She was three hours behind me on the West Coast and I hoped she was still awake. I had no idea what time it was. I told her I needed help. She called me right away and I crumpled again. I told her what I remembered. Lisa carried me that night. She stayed with me. She listened and supported me. She knew I would be all right. Whatever had taken her to bed earlier had passed a couple of hours before and she was now fine. She knew that it was coming for me too. I wouldn't have made it through this first night without her love and support.

Eventually, I locked up the house and went upstairs to bed. Lisa told me to take all of my heart rocks from Sedona and put them around my bed. Create a protective barrier of love from all the love I had found in my life. I crawled into bed and Sophie nestled in right next to my face. She gently licked my hand and arm to help calm me. Finnegan checked on me, went to the doorway and laid in front of it. They were both protecting me. As I drifted off to sleep, I felt my dad holding me tight as he would when I was a little girl and had had a particularly bad dream. He stayed with me then and was staying with me now. He was with me all night. He was with me always.

CHAPTER NINETEEN

Finding Release

I woke up the next morning feeling like I had been beaten up or hit by a truck. Every muscle in my body ached and I was exhausted. My emotions were raw and burning. I was fragile and vulnerable. It was almost exactly nine months after that day on the beach in Santa Barbara to recover this block of memory. It appeared I now had a new birthday, March 24, 2014, forty-seven years and eleven days following my original one. All of the sudden, my life made sense. I was conflicted. I was feeling a sense of shock and horror regarding what I had recalled, yet a huge sense of relief and gratitude that I had finally broken through this barrier. I lay motionless as I listened to soft music. I wondered - what do I do now?

Leaning Out

I had made my first climb up Cathedral Rock around this time five years ago. I had explored and realized all of the blockages that lived within me. Now it was time to take one more climb. Not up the rock, but into the light and freedom on the other side of this darkness that had lived within me. I had the pieces of my life's puzzle. As I crawled out of bed and took those first tentative steps, I decided to first honor my heart and spirit. I used all four Native American medicinal herbs to smudge the house. I burned sage to purify, cedar to protect, sweet grass to attract positive energies, and tobacco to create and offer prayers of respect and gratitude. I opened the windows and let the cold Cleveland air rush in and clear out the stale, stagnant energy. I knew no harm would come to me. I was safe, protected, and loved.

I had a coaching call scheduled with Lynn later that morning. She knew immediately that I was in distress. We talked through where I was right now. She asked me what we needed to do, and how she could help. I needed help to create a system, a process to deal with this. I asked her to be the keeper of questions. There were things I needed to explore or consider. I trusted her and her instinct to know exactly when to ask me and help me draw something into my awareness. I asked her to help me keep my mind in a steady cadence and encourage my emotions.

I asked Lynn to be my objective perspective. We discussed the potential need for therapy. It wasn't outside of my consideration. There was no question that I was in a delicate emotional space. However, this felt different to me compared to other moments in my past. I was being lifted by this experience. I didn't feel as if I were descending or needing help to be pulled out of something. I was climbing out and I had people there holding the rope. As long as I was climbing and not descending or falling, I was good. It felt as if everything I had worked on for the past fifteen years was preparing me for this exact moment. I wanted to stay my course a little while. We agreed to check in on this point.

We created a schedule to support me as I navigated those first, crucial days. We had daily "check-in" sessions. We set mini-goals and assignments for me between our calls. Lynn set forward motion with me and kept me accountable.

My third call was to Lisa. There were no words to express my gratitude for what she had given me the night before. She was my rock and shoulder. In those first days, she cared for me and told me when to fix something soft and warm to eat, to take a break and rest, or to soak in a warm salt bath.

She was a conduit to my past. I took maternal strength and energy from her as I listened to her engage with her seven-year-old son. She helped me find my laughter. We found moments in almost every conversation where we reverted to two crazy teenaged girls talking about boys, shoes, hair, and shopping. Lisa gave me laughter in the tears and reminded me of the beautiful power of this emotion and unconditional friendship.

Where I once would have sought isolation in such moment, I instead sought comfort in those I trusted. For the first time in my life, I intentionally and willfully leaned out. I created a system around me of people who supported and honored me as I worked through my process. They made me feel safe, protected, and loved. They were the keepers of details; they allowed me to experience it as I needed. They let me be whoever I needed to be and listened without judgment. They supported my emotions. I wasn't left on the other side of a slammed door. The door was finally open and there were arms waiting to support me and move me through the process. I kept as physically active as I could. Running was a major release mechanism, and I called upon it to keep my body flowing as I worked through my emotions. I balanced it with rest, and took comfort every night as Sophie curled up by my head, Finnegan on guard at the door, and my dad watching over me as I slept.

I allowed myself to be whoever I was. I cycled through my memories and at times it felt as if I was being spun on a tilt-a-whirl ride that had lost control. I was dizzy and nauseous as my heart and head tried to find center. Each cycle brought additional understanding, recall, and emotion. I started to connect the dots of my life, every action, reaction, and mechanism was tied to the protective force within me. Now I was freeing myself, and I wanted to be released as quickly as possible.

On the second night, I had a dream. I was standing on the shore of a beautiful beach. I hadn't been there before. The waves were enormous and I was in the water as they crashed to the shore. I was screaming at the top of my lungs. I don't know what I was saying. My dream seemed to simultaneously take me to another beach as a little girl with my dad. I was born with fallen ankles, and the doctors had said that running on the sand would help build the muscles in my feet and legs. My dad used to take me to Huntington Beach. He chided me to run, play tag, and chase after things. I ran out to the end of the pier and chased the sea gulls. When I was tired, we sat on the sand or the rock pier and he told me about the waves. He said the waves were nature's way of carrying away the bad things. Any time I had something I wanted to get rid of, all I had to do was wait for the wave to come in and give it what I didn't want anymore. It would scoop up my "bad" and pull it to the bottom. I could do this as much as I needed, until I was sure it was all gone. The waves would keep coming and take it all away.

As the adult on this new beach in my dream, I was allowing those massive waves to pull all the "bad" to the bottom of the deepest ocean. I could feel the undercurrent pull at my legs as the water rushed around me and swept everything underneath. I heard the waves crash repeatedly and consistently as I screamed. I wasn't there alone. There was a man. He was not my father, and I felt that his love for me was deep and unbounded. I felt him behind me, watching me as I was in the water. At just the right moment, he came up to me, and told me he would be there for me forever. I awoke feeling relief and comfort, along with faith that something beautiful was in the offing.

An Introduction

The next morning, I sat at my desk and wrote Lynn an email. I suspended my writing until I had a better handle on everything. I looked out the window and saw something. It was a bundle of energy that felt like a little girl. She was frightened and bewildered. She seemed to need comfort and I asked her if she wanted to come in. She nodded yes, and silently took a seat in my office. I wasn't certain what was happening but given the events of the past few days, nothing was beyond possibility.

I told her everything was going to be all right. I would help her. I asked her what was wrong? She told me she had to figure out what to do. She had made a mess and needed to fix it before she got into trouble. She couldn't meet my eyes; they were focused on her bound hands. I asked her what made her feel like she was in trouble and she said simply, "Because I let you remember." The wind went out of my lungs. I looked at her and realized who she was. Sitting before me was the mastermind of that survivor's instinct. She was the first version of my ego, the protector within me. She was me. She was ten.

I told her it would be all right and we would figure this out together. I was there to protect her now. She could relax. It broke my heart to see she didn't know how to do that. She sat forward in the chair and kept looking around as if to keep an eye out for something. I tried to keep myself as calm as possible as I waited anxiously for my call with Lynn. I wasn't sure what was happening, and I knew Lynn would help me find my course with the unexpected arrival of my ten-year-old self. Lynn considered what I told her and asked me if I had heard of *Active Imagination*[11]. It's a subconscious visualization process defined by Carl Jung. I hadn't, but I was curious, and I was open to anything. Please, tell me more.

In lay terms, *Active Imagination* is a meditative technique that can be used to bridge conversation between the conscious and the unconscious aspects of the mind. It allows us to engage our subconscious and allow it to share at its own will without interference. The intention is that through this process, the unconscious will inform the conscious mind, and thus become more whole. It's a way that may help us suspend the barrier of our conscious memory that is the keeper of things we may not want to know. The little girl had appeared, and I was curious to know everything about her. I wanted to help her feel less afraid. Active Imagination might help save us both.

The first step was to draw the little girl. This gave me a visual and physical context to the energy. It took me ten minutes to draw her the first time. I cried for a long time as I realized who she was, what she had endured, and how difficult it must have been for her to keep all of this from me. She was tired, she was tough, she was young, she was fragile, and she was brave. In drawing her, she became *real* to me in a way that I needed at this moment. She became a distinctive energy, a brave little girl who spoke from a corner of my subconscious mind that had been long hidden from my conscious self.

I felt an instant sense of detachment from her, and yet an intense connection to my *purpose* with her. She was a child who needed my help. She desperately wanted to be heard, and yet she was terrified to speak. She had been my instinct and fear. She also had been my warrior. She was tattered and battered, but she still had fight. There was such tremendous fight within that sweet, delicate little girl.

Our first conversations were a little difficult, as it seemed we were both a bit timid and shy. I calmed myself into a meditative state and allowed my deeper subconscious to drive the process. I sat at my desk and wrote everything she told me. I looked straight out the window into the night. It took a couple of tries, but I settled into a space where I could let the words flow freely as they came from her voice onto the page. It was my job as the adult and the moderator to coax the information out of her in a way that kept her safe and assured her that she was safe. If she felt threatened, she'd shut down. It took her a few tries too.

Our first rule was that anything she told me was between us. I wouldn't tell anyone what she told me without her permission. She wasn't in trouble, and she had done nothing wrong. It was time for her to tell me. She was safe and I kept telling her she was. I wasn't going to let anything happen to her. She had held on for almost forty years and now the holds were loosening, the knots were giving way, and that was a good thing. She was a little girl, and she deserved to play, and be all the things a ten-year-old should be. After the many years she had protected me, it was my turn to protect her.

When I came out of a session, I reflected upon our conversation. Her mother, the one person she thought would trust and protect her, didn't believe her and didn't help her. That's why it was crucially important to be believed. She made sure we had the facts straight and could defend ourselves. She started to open up. She started to draw deeper, richer explanations around what had happened during those years at the townhouse. She set me straight on more than one occasion and was happy when she corrected me. She was bright and quite capable. She kept things highly organized and always had to know what came next. She always had a plan. She toed a very straight line and tried to stay just out of the mainstream of life in order to remain unnoticed. She did not like to be the center of attention. She shared her emotions in an almost matter-of-fact tone, and this touched me. She didn't have time to feel things, as she had to keep working on protecting. Eventually, we found our way to tears and then we cried openly and freely whenever it seemed right. At that point, it always seemed right.

She asked me one evening if we could talk during the daytime instead. She was afraid of the night. My mother had worked at night. She was a light sleeper because of this fear and always nervous sleeping in new places. Keep the closet door open and check it before bed. You can only close the closet door at night after you've checked it. That way, even if someone is in there who you hadn't seen, they would have to open the door to get to you and that would give you a minute to run.

She was much more descriptive during our day sessions. It was there where she revealed the more gruesome details. I was shocked by the graphic nature of her tone and choice in words. She told me as much as she could remember about every time it happened. As she shared, I could smell and taste everything as she described it to me. I could feel my body resisting, bracing, and reacting to what was happening. I felt profound pain in my body, and moments I was gasping for air. I was dizzy and nauseous. There were moments when I had to break away to vomit.

We had five daylight sessions in all, after which, I went for a long run or work out at the gym - anything to burn off the toxic evil. Every evening, I soaked in a warm salt bath and calmed myself. I ate simple foods like eggs and rice and drank ginger tea to keep my stomach settled. She told me when she wanted to rest and I always let her rest, no matter what time of day or night, and what else was going on. If this little girl needed it, she got it.

She liked to color and draw and I bought her crayons, charcoal, and a sketchpad. One of her first pictures was of a house and I asked where it was. She said, "It's our home silly, the place where we are happiest." I asked her what made her happy there and she said, "Because there are mountains and water in the same place and we can go to either anytime we want. It's warm and there are lots of people who love us and we love them. We are able to sleep at night to the sound of the waves and the air tastes and smells salty like tears. There aren't sad tears here. We only cry happy tears here." I asked her if we had lived there yet and she said, "No, but we will soon because it's almost over. It's the place I dream we will live and love more than anywhere. It's our home."

I had always slept with the help of white noise in the form of rainfall sounds for years. I asked her if she would like it if we started listening to waves instead. She said yes. I asked her if she remembered what Daddy told us about the waves. She said yes, and wondered if we could go to the beach. So we did. We sat on the pier and looked out over the water. We listened to music, made prayers, and let things go little by little. It was at the beach where I allowed the seven-year-old, the heart, to interact a bit. The ten-year-old protector was ever so slowly becoming a little girl again. The seven-year-old would show her the way.

After a few weeks, she felt more confident that I was capable of protecting us. I told her it was time to tell Mom what we knew. This frightened her, and I watched her grow strong to prepare for this battle. We agreed to write a letter. We didn't want to see her, and we didn't want to hear her say she didn't believe us again. We were going to be okay. We wanted to be free, but we didn't need to tell my mother in person. I let her write the first letter and she was allowed to use any word she wanted. I promised I would never share it with anyone; it was our secret. It was the one and only thing of hers that we wrote and destroyed. I let her burn it.

I wrote a second version that came from a place of adult anger. I unleashed my rage at the woman who did this to her child and expressed the disbelief I felt. It was the third version that came from both of us, and found its way to my mother's desk in her study. I knew this quite possibly could be the last communication I would ever have with my mother.

CHAPTER TWENTY

Finding Perspective

With the letter in my mother's hands, I was ready to sink deeper into my grieving. The ten-year-old had told most of her story and it was time to let her heal. I spent a great deal of time in reflection. I replayed my entire life and found the moments the ten-year-old jumped in front. I had a nearly complete timeline of my life and I slowly kept filling in the details. There were moments when reflection gave way to profound sadness and in this; I found an even deeper layer of pain and release. It was a cycle; and I spun quickly at first, and in time, it slowed.

Anger settled in and manifested as a massive respiratory infection. I had a horrible cough and was unable to speak for nearly a week. It appeared the harsh Cleveland winter caught me as it gave way to spring and brought me an opportunity to clear my throat chakra. Throat chakra represents expression and communication and it is where anger ultimately leaves. I was actually relieved to be sick. It meant I had reached another level of release and I was one step closer to an end. My anger and confusion spiraled around and stopped at one point – my mother. It seemed impossible to fathom any circumstance that would make her actions acceptable to me. I shifted from trying to understand to trying to find the appropriate place for this to live within me. It would always be a part of me.

My First Reframe

A painful realization emerged as I recalled the conversation with my doctors asking if I had been abused. Now that I remembered, I wondered. Was the extent and severity of internal damage and scar tissue consistent with sexual abuse? I had lived with the shame that I had somehow done this to myself. I believed it was my fault, that I had been somehow careless with my life and this choice. These circumstances no longer seemed valid as a new perspective emerged.

The timing of it all was tied to a big day on the calendar, Mother's Day. I stayed in deep reflection and grief. I recalled the day on my couch in that apartment, visiting the memorial, the stroller by the side of the creek. The physical pain I lived with, the drug treatments, the therapy to find context with this loss. I revisited all of this, reframed it in light of my new understanding. There was a lot of sleep balanced with physical movement. I was working through it with every fiber of my being. Both little girls were sad and recovering as well. I stayed quiet. I spent lots of time at the beach and on the swings. I needed comfort, rest, and quiet. I didn't watch any television, and I stayed inside a good deal. That was the one point where I kept a little more to myself as I sorted through my sadness and disbelief.

In the past, when my relationship with my mother was distressed, I found a way to honor her on Mother's Day. Not this year. This year I would honor another mother. I would honor me. The night before Mother's Day, I asked for a dream. I wondered if there was an opportunity to see my children, to know them in a way that I could see them but not disturb them. If in my asking for this dream it offered the smallest risk they would be harmed by my being there, I should not be allowed the dream. What I wanted was not worth risking their well-being or happiness. I knew only that they existed, somewhere out there in the universe.

I went to sleep and in this dream, I sat on a bench in a beautiful park. It was this rich, regal shade of green, with beds of flowers wrapped around big trees. There were thousands of tulips of all colors – red, white, and pink. Tulips are my favorite flower and I saw those as a sign of safety for the place where we were. There were swing sets and jungle gyms and a big sand box. A little pond sat just beyond with a trail that wrapped around and there were toy boats sailing on the water.

I heard them first. I heard laughter, lots of giggling, and a little sparring too. There were three of them. Two girls and a boy. He was younger and the girls were twins. They all had blonde hair and blue eyes. They were playing together and laughing all the while. The girls teased their brother and they pushed and pulled on each other. My girls looked exactly the same, except I could tell the difference, it was so slight, but it was there. My older one, she was the commander-in-chief, and I believe that was a self-proclaimed title as she was *technically* the oldest. I heard her offer this reminder to her other siblings a couple of times, and this was met with sideways glances and rolled eyes. My younger one was a bit wistful and easily distracted. She seemed to giggle more than anything and it would be difficult for her to stay mad at anything for any great period of time. She seemed to want to do whatever pleased her at the moment without too much concern.

My girls were on the swings and challenging each other to jump off and see who could go farther. I smiled, as I knew exactly where that came from. My boy was a little quiet and seemed a bit shy, but he had a beautiful smile and his face lit up when he heard his sisters teasing. I think he was grateful that they were at each other and giving him a break. He seemed happy to be with himself as well as with his sisters. He was handsome and adorable.

I sat quietly as I watched them. I was careful to not disrupt this energy, as I was an extra special guest in the place that was their home. I wondered who kept watch over them and saw big almost fairy-like stars that hovered gently but intently overhead. They kept my children in check and allowed them their time to be free and wistful. I smiled as they tumbled around on the grass and kicked a ball around the field. My heart caught as I watched them swinging like monkeys on the jungle gym. I kept a watchful eye to make sure they didn't fall. My son had a little boat and I heard him saying he wanted to go over to the pond and play with it in the water. My daughters wanted nothing to do with that just yet. They wanted to finish the game they were playing and then they would go to the water with him. They promised and asked him to come help them finish their game of kickball. He shrugged his shoulders and rolled his eyes as he said okay, I think knowing that he was always going to be under their direction. He didn't seem to mind. He was such a gentle soul. I knew that would make my son a great man one day.

I looked over on the bench and saw my Dad. I wasn't sure when he had shown up, but he was next to me and holding my hand. He said that he checked in from time to time just to be sure they were all right. He hadn't done anything to disturb them on his visits, and he was proud of me for being so loving and protective of them. He thought that soon they would be leaving here to go where their lives would next take them. He was glad that I had been able to come and see them.

We sat there quietly. After awhile he told me it was probably time to head back and I nodded. I watched as they slowly started kicking the ball toward the pond. I whispered that I loved them. Be safe and well and kind. Do any great thing you wish in this life, believe in yourself most of all, and know always that you are loved. You are loved so very much. My son called out that it was time to sail a little toy boat, and he turned and looked at me and smiled. I saw the twinkle in his eye. My Dad squeezed my hand and said, "Happy Mother's Day, Sunshine" and with that I woke up with tears streaming down my face and a great smile. I stared into the darkness and I was overcome with happiness and sadness at the same time.

When I awoke in the morning, I stayed in bed for a while and listened to some gentle music. I was in no hurry and eventually got up, made my breakfast, and enjoyed a quiet cup of tea. I went to the gym to work out and stopped at the grocery on the way home. I picked up things for my dinner, my special healthy twist on mac and cheese – quinoa and cheese with peas - along with fresh vegetables for a salad and vanilla meringues for dessert. I had a bottle of pinot noir at home that I was saving for a special occasion. Today was it.

I went to the flower area to pick up some fresh flowers. What called to me strongly were purple calla lilies. I was drawn to their delicate beauty and the sense of strength they also seemed to carry. I picked up two bunches. As I held them, I thought immediately of a wedding, my wedding. I thought of my children giving them to me, it was like they had picked them out. When I arrived home, I researched their meaning. The calla lily is appropriate for any occasion that involves major transition, rebirth, or new beginnings. Calla lilies are a favorite in wedding ceremonies and by contrast are often used on the graves of young children who died too young or suffered an untimely death. I found this perfectly fitting and completely beautiful.

A New Voice

With Mother's Day behind me, it was time to focus on the final chapter of school. I was completing my coaching certification. Summer was almost here, and I could feel the days growing longer and the sun shining a little brighter. It stayed cool when the wind blew from the north across the lake. It was perfect running weather and I was shedding layers – physically and emotionally.

In June, I flew to Santa Barbara to complete the coaching certification program. I revisited the spot on the familiar beach and reflected upon all I had experienced in the past year. I brought the heart rock I found on at the beach that morning, a year before. It had broken into four pieces shortly after I moved to Cleveland. I was the only person on this public beach and the water was gentle and calm. I walked into the water far enough to feel the pull of the current. Then, one piece at a time, I allowed the ocean in its gentle way to carry that heart out to sea. As I walked along the water's edge after, I found two new heart rocks. They weren't that far away from each other and when I held them in my hand, they nested together.

My last school session started the next morning. This special group of people would rise up to support me one more time. We went around the circle and were asked to share the pivotal moment of this program. I considered what I would share, I had it all picked out, and then something odd happened.

One of my closer friends shared about her father, how much she had been missing him, how much he had meant to her and how much she felt his presence as she achieved this milestone and task. I was moved to tears and paused to consider my own father and how I hoped he would be proud of this moment for me as well. Then a few moments later, another close friend spoke up. She stunned me as she shared with the group how much this journey had enlightened her, brought her into a deeper understanding of herself and finding her way in this life. How she had realized at LifeLaunch™ that she had been standing next to a victim, and how she was struck with how the universe brings people together. How being there allowed her to open up to others, and the profound healing that was always within reach. I was sitting in front of her on the floor. I was crying. She looked at me when she was finished and said, "Good luck" and everybody laughed. I stared at her and she nodded. It was my turn.

I was able to tell the room that in case they were wondering, I was the victim that had been standing next to her. I paused for a long time. I took about six deep cleansing breaths. I knew that this was my moment, my first moment to say out loud what I had been processing for less than three months. I had written, I had shared privately, but if I was going to get this out there needed to be a first time. I was safe in that room. We had been asked to keep a journal and submit it as a part of our course work. I included part of my experience in that journal. When I felt I could speak, I looked up and around the room. My eyes settled first on my group mentor, and then on Pam McLean, the founder of the Hudson Institute. I knew she had read my journal. She was the steadiest rock and held space wide open for me. She allowed me and I trusted her. I kept my eyes on her and in a small voice said, "March 24, 2014. The night I remembered everything I needed to know to finally set myself free. I wouldn't have been able to do that had it not been for all of this. Thank you." I smiled at my friend and said a silent, "Thank you for helping me get there." The next morning, I passed my final exam, received my certification, and celebrated with that amazing group of people.

A Moment at the Creek

I set off to Sedona to regroup, celebrate, and imagine what would come next. Lisa joined me for a few days and it was wonderful to share this beautiful place with someone who had brought me such comfort and support in these recent weeks. We explored some of my favorite spots. One morning we went to the Oak Creek at Crescent Moon Ranch. It's the starting point for the hike up Cathedral Rock and I took my crystals to a favorite spot to wash them. As I pulled the crystals out of my pack, my garnet and star ruby flipped into the water immediately and rested upon a ledge. I had used those crystals for work on my root and sacral chakras. It had happened before with other crystals at other points of my journey, I looked at them, and wondered if they were ready to be released. If a crystal flipped into the water, it was a good indication that it was time to let it go. They were sitting on a little rock ledge and I left them there while I cleared out the rest.

I took the two rogue crystals and placed each in my hand, and allowed the creek's current to gently carry them away. After the last crystal caught the current and went into the creek, my entire root and sacral areas went into a spasm. I had never experienced anything like that before. My instinct told me to put my hands and feet into the water and center myself using the current and the stability of the red rock on my back. My feet were far enough in that they could feel the current of the creek. I felt a gentle sweeping motion and felt the creek help me clear whatever remained in these chakras.

Lisa was again a patient friend as I worked through this step. I stayed until the spasm subsided and my body felt at total ease. We started packing up and a piece of aquamarine flipped into the creek. I turned around and an older gentleman appeared almost as if from out of nowhere. He had a camera and was looking for some photo opportunities and a cool, shady spot to enjoy his lunch. I offered him my favorite spot by the creek, and gave him some possible spots for great pictures. He saw the aquamarine in the creek and asked me if I wanted to take it. I said no, it seemed happy where it was for the moment so I let it be.

Lisa and I set off down the trail and eventually turned back for the car. It was on our way back when we came across the man we met at the creek. He was smiling, almost grateful that he had found us. He handed me the piece of aquamarine. He said that after I left the crystal jumped out of the water and into his hand. He was a little freaked by it but he knew he was supposed make sure that I had it. He said, "Whoever he is, he didn't want you to leave him behind." I smiled and thanked him, and wished him well. I met his eyes and felt a familiarity toward him. I realized later I hadn't asked his name, but if I had to guess, I'd bet it was David.

Father's Day

Lisa left the next morning and I had a few days on my own. Father's Day was approaching and I planned to write a blog post in honor of my dad. In getting ready, I asked the little girls what they wanted to say and the ten-year-old popped up and wanted to tell me what she knew about "that" night. Was she allowed to tell? I said of course and in that she revealed one last story. This one chronicled the days leading up to my father's death, the night he died, and the days immediately following. She filled in blanks and was certain he didn't commit suicide. She wanted me to know that there was no way my dad would have ever left me. He's with us always, protecting us the best way he can from where he is. He didn't leave willingly or intentionally. I looked out at the stars, at a beautiful full moon as I slowly began to reframe another moment and take another step forward.

CHAPTER TWENTY-ONE

Last Stop - The Beach

Back in Cleveland, and after finishing the first draft of this book, they wanted to go to the beach. Huntington Beach has been a part of my young life and a pivotal part on this journey home. We sat on the pier and the ten-year-old looked out over the water. The seven-year-old took off to the end of the pier. She was whooping at the sea gulls and flapping along with them. I watched to make sure she didn't fall in. Smiling, I turned back to the older one. She asked me what would happen now. I told her I thought we should celebrate a little. She looked at me a little quizzically and asked me, "Do you mean like a party?"

I told her sort of like that, that we would find the right way. I told her that I was abundantly proud of who she was; that she had to experience things that are beyond what anyone can imagine. She had opened up to me and trusted me, and I knew it was a struggle for her to do that. She had shared her feelings, shown me anger and fear. She showed how she had protected us for all of these years, and how we survived. How she had found the strength, courage and will to keep moving.

She was the victim, the warrior, and the hero all at the same time, all rolled into one amazing, beautiful little girl. She was a warrior in the greatest sense of the word. She made war, not for evil but in order to survive. She fought demons and held them at bay, and now we were ready to let them go. They will face their own destiny and we could go and live our life happy, clear, and free.

She considered this and asked me if she was going to die? I said no. "No sweetie, you are not going to die. There is a part of you that you don't need to worry about anymore and that might feel a little like dying might, but you are very much alive, and it is time to play. That part of you that might feel as if it is dying is the part that is scared all of the time. That part of you that lived every day not exactly sure if you would get hurt. The part of you that doesn't want to trust anyone, and is afraid to take a chance that someone will be there for you and they would care for you. These are all parts that you don't need anymore. We will work together to find forgiveness and gratitude and let those go."

I assured her that we will walk forward into our life as a peaceful warrior, wounded but not defeated. We will sit with a quiet assurance and a steady confidence in who we are and what we bring to the people we love. We have scars. These scars are our quiet reminder of the journey we led, and our undeniable courage to keep fighting and keep trying. We don't need to forget, and you, you don't need to be concerned with protecting us. That is my job now.

I looked up and the seven-year-old was screaming with delight and running back down the pier toward us. She stopped dead in her tracks and asked me, what we were going to do now? I asked her what she wanted to do. She got a big grin on her face and she said quickly that she wanted to swing. Swing high and jump far. I nodded and said, "Okay, let's go." And with that, the seven-year-old grabbed the hand of the ten-year-old. It was the first time I noticed. The ties that had bound her hands, they had frayed away, the last threads dangling from her wrists and falling away as the seven-year-old tugged at her. The little girl was free, released. Untethered.

The seven-year-old had to pull her to her feet and encourage her along those first steps. I heard her moan "Come on." The way a child says it when they want you to get it and join in. The ten-year-old glanced back at me. I saw her eyes. They were willful and a bit cautious, but they were shining. I smiled and winked at her and nodded for her to go on. I looked up as I saw the ten-year-old break into a run. I heard her laugh all the while holding hands with the seven-year-old. She turned around and asked me if I was coming, she was wearing a smile I had never seen. Her hands were waving at me freely in the air.

George Elliot said, "It's never too late to be what you might have been." To me, it says that you should never let go of your dreams, never underestimate the spirit and magic of the universe, and never, ever give up on you, for you are the catalyst to your own destiny.

I waved back and pulled myself up from the pier to follow them. I stopped and watched them barrel up the stairs to the swings. I heard the seven-year-old say, "It's my turn to pick the swing first because you got to go first last time."

EPILOGUE

"Every new beginning comes from some
other beginning's end." – Seneca

Thank you for reading my story.

I love this quote from Seneca. To me, it's the way life works and it reminds me of my sunrise morning at Haleakala in Maui. There's the briefest moment when it's night and day at the same time. The sun works all night to find its' way back across the horizon and we don't see it until we experience dawn. This is that moment for me. I feel that I'm at an end of a long journey and yet at the threshold of something completely new and unknown. I'm eager and a little scared. It's not a fear for protection, it is a fear laced with excitement at what happens next. It's like having butterflies and goose bumps at the same time, all the time.

My goal in writing was to share my experience, not as a prescriptive, but rather as an example of the possibility that exists within each of us to change if we choose. My wish is this: if you are in a space of transition or considering changes to your life's direction or choices, you have found something here that may somehow compel you on your journey. I said to myself at the outset that if I were able to touch one life, in one way, that helped or healed, then my mission would be fulfilled.

Many of the techniques and methods I have shared were experienced with the assistance of highly skilled practitioners and experts. If you have any interest in exploring any of the concepts set out in this story, I encourage you to seek out appropriate professional guidance.

I realized something along my journey. I came to trust that I was my own, most powerful secret weapon. Change came from within me, because of me, because that person who lived within my very core wanted to get somewhere in life. I learned how to believe and lean into others and the universe. I learned how to embrace the magic and believe in myself most of all.

In many ways, my story is ending and it's also just beginning. I have accomplished many of my goals and sit here with an impassioned perspective and purpose. However, I see life as a cycle and, for as much as I've learned, I know there is still a lot more out there to experience, and I remain a curious explorer.

I wanted to leave you with a few notes in case you were wondering how far I had come since the ending of the book:

I continue to recover memories. These memories are filling in gaps and bringing additional detail forward. None have been as violent as that night in March. The memories aren't always pleasant, yet they continue to complete a timeline and this is a part of the process that I have grown to accept.

The ten-year-old continues to learn how to be less of a boss and more of a little girl. She yields to me more and more and is less fearful with respect to life. Some of her habits and mechanisms have been in place for decades and they won't go away overnight. However, I have a far greater awareness and am learning how to spot my reactions to situations and interactions, and I keep learning.

I'm allowing some things to remain with me. I believe we are shaped by our experiences and it is not necessary to forget. In fact, there are things

I can't forget. What I have been able to do is find perspective around my experiences and find a way to allow them to live peacefully within me. I don't need to be defined by them. In allowing this, I now accept that it is possible that I may always be a little skittish in new situations and around new people. I may always have trouble sleeping in strange places. It may be difficult for me to be around anger and big emotion(s). I may need a little help when I'm trying to express my emotions. In accepting that those things may always live within me, I also accept that they may diminish in their strength and some may fall away altogether. Such is the course of life.

I'm a recovering workaholic and this addiction will live in my shadow for the rest of my life. The shadow is the part of me that's filled with my less desirable aspects and qualities, and it is another dimension of my uniqueness and imperfection as a human being and as an individual. When it tugs and asks to get out in front, it's an opportunity for me to pause and check in with intentions and goals. I don't need to hide from it, but rather learn and embrace what lives in it. I honor the things that helped me survive and what that has taught and brought me. I'll remember that I'm made of both darkness and light. The sun works all night to come across the horizon and the shadow falls behind when we face it.

We are the sum of our experiences and it makes us messy. I think it's the mess that makes us absolute beautiful, and special treasures. There is a grace that emerges from imperfection. I was amazed at what happened the moment I let go of my expectations to achieve and simply experienced what was available to me. As I became more transparent and real about all of me – good and bad – the world seemed to open around me.

The little girls play together and the heart teaches the protector how to stand down and have fun. We color. We go to the beach and chase the seagulls off the end of the pier. We've never met a swing we didn't like.

As we reach higher and higher into the sky with each swing, I think about the Hawaiian word *aloha*. It means hello, good-bye, and love. Aloha and more specifically the Aloha way is more than a greeting or expression of affection, it's a way of being and living. To live in Aloha is to be in the presence of life, to revel and share its essence of being with openness, honesty, and humility. It is a commitment to being real. It reminds us that love is all around us. It reminds us to embrace it, manifest it and share it with someone, starting and ending with you, and then begin again. Then watch as the world lights the way to possibility and joy.

Aloha

ABOUT THE AUTHOR

Kate is an author, speaker, certified coach, and recovering workaholic. She is a seasoned entrepreneur and has worked extensively with companies of all size and scale as they navigate the complexities and challenges of growth and development. She has particular expertise working with small businesses and business owners as they carve a path to exit and search for the "next" in their lives.

She helps individuals seeking greater depth, perspective, and balance. Her coaching practice focuses on the "adult" children living abusive histories and how survival mechanisms manifest into addictive and/or co-dependent behaviors. She speaks on the influence of these behaviors from personal and organizational perspectives.

Kate earned a Bachelor of Arts and a Master in Business Administration from Baldwin-Wallace University in Berea, Ohio. She is a certified meditator and received her coaching certification from the Hudson Institute of Santa Barbara, California.

She is an avid runner and hiker and when she's not out on the trail, you'll find her in the kitchen cooking or at the ballpark. Kate's a curious adventurer in life, with a pinch of gypsy to keep it interesting. She considers the world her playground and has never met a swing she didn't like.

Additional contact information can be found in the References and Resources section of this book.

REFERENCES AND RESOURCES

Please visit the website www.kateelizebethnagel.com for the latest on books, articles, and other media and resources related to the ideas and issues discussed in this story. It's my intention to create an online discussion around key topics such as workaholism, suicide and depression, and sexual abuse as well as transformative change and active imagination. I invite you to share your experiences with this story and your journey. Drop me an email at kate@kateelizebethnagel.com, @KateENagel on Twitter and/or follow my author page, at Untethered – Kate Elizebeth Nagel, on Facebook.

Cover photography provided by Bill Willson. For more information regarding his portfolio and services, please connect with Bill at www.billwillson.com.

END NOTES

[1]   Chapter 7: References to autoimmune disease, endometriosis begins here. Endometriosis is a condition where tissue similar to the lining of the uterus, which should only be located inside the uterus, is found elsewhere in the body. These cells become trapped and can adhere to other internal organs, most commonly ovaries and intestinal organs. The web-site www.endometriosis.org has detailed information on the disease, symptoms and causes, and treatments.

[2]   Chapter 11: References to chakra, chakra energy, and chakra healing are my consolidated interpretations based upon my own knowledge as well as information reviewed from a number of websites including: www.wikipedia.org/wiki/Chakra, August, 2014; www.mindbodygreen.com/0-91/The-7-Chakras-for-Beginners.html, September, 2014; and www.threeheartscompany.com/chakra.html, September, 2014.

[3]   Chapter 12: Ibid.

[4]   Chapter 12: The concept of the peaceful warrior is based, in part, on the works of Dan Millman. More information can be found at www.peacefulwarrior.com. The use of this terminology is to reflect a balanced approach to navigating conflict in ones life.

[5]   Part Four Introduction: Quote from Albert Einstein originally appeared in an obituary published in Life Magazine, May 2, 1955 by William Miller. Miller recalled the advice Einstein gave his son, "Try not to become a man of success, but try rather to become a man of value." Inclusion permitted by the Albert Einstein Archives, Hebrew University of Jerusalem, Jerusalem 91904 Israel, November 20, 2014.

[6] Chapter 15: References to the Oklahoma City Memorial, www. oklahomacitynationalmemorial.org, March, 2014.

[7] Chapter 16: References to crystal meanings and properties are based upon my own knowledge and learnings as well as information reviewed from a number of websites including: www.meanings.crystalsandjewelry.com, October, 2014; and www.crystal-cure.com, October, 2014

[8] Chapter 17: References to the raven are based upon my own knowledge and learnings as well as information reviewed from the following web-site: www.whats-your-sign.com, September, 2014

[9] Chapter 17: In addition to the crystal meaning references used in Chapter 16, www.jademeaning.com, October, 2014 was reviewed.

[10] Chapter 18: References to the turkey vulture are based upon my own knowledge as well as information reviewed from the following web-site: www.whats-your-sign.com, June, 2014

[11] Chapter 19: References to Active Imagination and Carl Jung were interpreted from the following sources: http://en.wikipedia.org/wiki/Active_imagination, September, 2014 and http://www.jung.org, September, 2014

CPSIA information can be obtained at www.ICGtesting.com
Printed in the USA
BVOW08s0210270315

393609BV00001B/41/P